4

College Oral
Communication

College Oral Communication

**HOUGHTON MIFFLIN
ENGLISH FOR ACADEMIC SUCCESS**

Steve Jones

Community College of Philadelphia

SERIES EDITORS

Patricia Byrd

Joy M. Reid

Cynthia M. Schuemann

Houghton Mifflin Company

Boston   New York

Publisher: Patricia A. Coryell
Director of ESL Publishing: Susan Maguire
Senior Development Editor: Kathy Sands Boehmer
Editorial Assistant: Evangeline Bermas
Senior Project Editor: Kathryn Dinovo
Manufacturing Assistant: Karmen Chong
Senior Marketing Manager: Annamarie Rice

Cover graphics: LMA Communications, Natick, Massachusetts

Photo credits: © Charles O'Rear/Corbis, p. 1; Purchase, Joseph Pulitzer Bequest, 1947 (47.11.5). Photograph, all rights reserved, The Metropolitan Museum of Art, p. 8; © Gianni Dagli Orti/Corbis, p. 19; © Condé Nast Archive/Corbis, p. 32; © Reuters/Corbis, p. 33; © Tim Pannell/Corbis, p. 33; Getty Images, p. 38; © CinemaPhoto/Corbis, p. 57; © LA Daily News/David Crane/Corbis Sygma, p. 57; © Joel Toner/*Horticultural Magazine*, p. 63; © Royalty-Free/Corbis, p. 89, © Patrik Giardino/Corbis, p. 103; © Eric K. K. Yu/Corbis, p. 121; © Penni Gladstone/San Francisco Chronicle/Corbis, p. 125; © Rob Lewine/Corbis, p. 148; © Royalty-Free/Corbis, p. 154, © Tom Stewart/Corbis, p. 166; © Dex Images, Inc./ Corbis, p. 168

Text credits: Frank J. Frost, *Greek Society*, Fifth Edition. Copyright © 1997 by Houghton Mifflin Company. Reprinted with permission, p. 11; Douglas Bernstein, *Essentials of Psychology*, Second Edition. Copyright © 2002 by Houghton Mifflin Company. Reprinted with permission, p. 37; www.cheaptickets.com. Reprinted with permission, p. 67; William Pride and O. C. Ferrell, *Marketing: Concepts and Strategies*, Twelfth Edition. Copyright © 2003 by Houghton Mifflin Company. Reprinted with permission, p. 70; Ethel Wood and Judith Lloyd Yero, *Introduction to Sociology*. Copyright © 2002 by McDougal Littell, Inc. Reprinted with permission, p. 101

Printed in the U.S.A.

Library of Congress Control Number: 2004112258

ISBN: 0-618-23019-X

123456789-CRW-08 07 06 05 04

Contents

Houghton Mifflin English for Academic Success Series

SERIES EDITORS

Patricia Byrd, Joy M. Reid, Cynthia M. Schuemann

☐ What Is the Purpose of This Series?

The Houghton Mifflin English for Academic Success series is a comprehensive program of student and instructor materials: four levels of student language proficiency textbooks in three skill areas (oral communication, reading, and writing), with supplemental vocabulary textbooks at each level. For instructors and students, a useful website supports classroom teaching, learning and assessment. For instructors, four Essentials of Teaching Academic Language books, (*Essentials of Teaching Academic Oral Communication, Essentials of Teaching Academic Reading, Essentials of Teaching Academic Writing*, and *Essentials of Teaching Academic Vocabulary*) provide helpful information for instructors new to teaching oral communication, reading, writing, and vocabulary.

The fundamental purpose of the series is to prepare students who are not native speakers of English for academic success in U.S. college degree programs. By studying these materials, students in college English-for-Academic-Purposes (EAP) courses will gain the academic language skills they need to be successful students in degree programs. Additionally, students will learn about being successful students in U.S. college courses.

The series is based on considerable prior research as well as our own investigations of students' needs and interests, instructors' needs and desires, and institutional expectations and requirements. For example, our survey research revealed what problems instructors feel they face in their classrooms and what they actually teach; who the students are and what they know and do not know about the "culture" of U.S. colleges; and what types of exams are required for admission at various colleges.

Student Audience

The materials in this series are for college-bound ESL students at U.S. community colleges and undergraduate programs at other institutions. Some of these students are U.S. high school graduates. Some of them are long-term U.S. residents who graduated from a high school before coming to the United States. Others are newer U.S. residents. Still others are more typical international students. All of them need to develop academic language skills and knowledge of ways to be successful in U.S. college degree courses.

All of the books in this have been created to implement the Houghton Mifflin English for Academic Success competencies. These competencies are based on those developed by ESL instructors and administrators in Florida, California, and Connecticut to be the underlying structure for EAP courses at colleges in those states. These widely respected competencies assure that the materials meet the real world needs of EAP students and instructors.

All of the books focus on . . .

- Starting where the students are, building on their strengths and prior knowledge (which is considerable, if not always academically relevant), and helping students self-identify needs and plans to strengthen academic language skills
- Academic English, including development of Academic Vocabulary and grammar required by students for academic speaking/listening, reading, and writing
- Master Student Skills, including learning style analysis, strategy training, and learning about the "culture" of U.S. colleges, which lead to their becoming successful students in degree courses and degree programs
- Topics and readings that represent a variety of academic disciplinary areas so that students learn about the language and content of the social sciences, the hard sciences, education, and business as well as the humanities

All of the books provide

- Interesting and valuable content that helps the students develop their knowledge of academic content as well as their language skills and student skills
- A wide variety of practical classroom-tested activities that are easy to teach and engage the students

▪ Assessment tools at the end of each chapter so that instructors have easy-to-implement ways to assess student learning and students have opportunities to assess their own growth

▪ Websites for the students and for the instructors: the student sites will provide additional opportunities to practice reading, writing, listening, vocabulary development, and grammar. The instructor sites will provide instructor's manuals, teaching notes and answer keys, value-added materials like handouts and overheads that can be reproduced to use in class, and assessment tools such as additional tests to use beyond the assessment materials in each book.

☐ What Is the Purpose of the Oral Communication Strand?

The oral communication strand of Houghton Mifflin English for Academic Success focuses on development of speaking and listening skills necessary for college study. Dedicated to meeting academic needs of students by teaching them how to handle the spoken English used by instructors and students in college classrooms, the four books provide engaging activities to practice both academic listening and academic speaking. Students learn to participate effectively in a variety of academic situations, including discussions, lectures, student study groups, and office meetings with their college instructors.

Because of the importance of academic vocabulary in the spoken English of the classroom, the oral communication strand teaches the students techniques for learning and using new academic vocabulary, both to recognize the words when they hear them and to use the words in their own spoken English. Grammar appropriate to the listening and speaking activities is also included in each chapter. For example, Book 2 includes work with the pronunciation of irregular past tense verbs as part of learning how to listen to and participate in academic discussions focused on history. In addition to language development, the books provide for academic skill development through the teaching of appropriate academic tasks and the giving of master student tips to help students better understand what is expected of them in college classes. Students learn to carry out academic tasks in ways that are linguistically, academically, and culturally appropriate. For example, students learn how to take information from the spoken presentations by their instructors and then to use that information for other academic tasks such as tests or small group discussions. That is, students are not taught to take notes for some abstract reason but learn to make a powerful connection between note-taking and success in other assigned tasks.

Each book has a broad disciplinary theme to give coherence to the content. These themes were selected because of their high interest for students; they are also topics commonly explored in introductory college courses and so provide useful background for students. Materials were selected that are academically appropriate but that do not require expert knowledge by the instructor. The following themes are used: Book 1: Human Behavior, Book 2: The Connections between Human Beings and Animals, Book 3: Communication and Media, and Book 4: Economics and Business. For example, Book 1 has one chapter about the psychological effects of music and another on the relationship between nutrition and psychological well-being. Book 2 uses topics such as taboo foods, animals as workers, using animals in medical and scientific testing along with one of Aesop's fables. Book 3 includes the history of movies, computer animation, privacy rights, and other topics related to modern media. Book 4 takes on a topic that fascinates most students with various themes related to money and finance, including such related topics as the history of money, marketing use of psychological conditioning, and the economics of the World Wide Web. These topics provide high-interest content for use in the listening and speaking activities, but do not require that instructors have to develop any new knowledge to be able to use the materials.

Instructor Support Materials

Recorded materials presented in each chapter are available on an audiotape or CD that is provided with each book. In addition to a recording of the main lecture for each chapter, the recording includes other materials such as dialogues and academic vocabulary.

The series also includes a resource book for instructors called *Essentials of Teaching Academic Oral Communication* by John Murphy. This practical book provides strategies and activities for the use of instructors new to the teaching of oral communication.

☐ What Is the Organization of *College Oral Communication 4?*

College Oral Communication 4 prepares advanced level students for the demands of college-level academic listening and speaking tasks. Six chapters of readings and lectures in history, psychology, e-commerce, sociology, biology, and literature present concepts and language that many students will encounter in future college courses.

Vocabulary is a prominent feature of the textbook. Each chapter provides a list of academic words related to the reading and lecture supported by pronunciation work in syllable number and stress.

Master Student Tips scattered throughout the textbook provide students with short comments on a particular strategy, activity, or practical advice to follow in an academic setting.

Chapter Organization

Each chapter is clearly divided into three sections: Effective Academic Listening, Effective Academic Speaking, and Assessing Your Academic Listening and Speaking Skills.

Effective Academic Listening

Getting Ready for Academic Listening Readings, charts and tables engage students in the content and prepare them to listen and take notes from lectures. Note-taking strategies such as recognizing signal words for different relationships between ideas, using symbols and abbreviations, and working with content vocabulary prepare students to listen and take notes from academic lectures and classroom communication.

Getting Information from the Lecture Students are guided toward successful note-taking by preparatory listening for content and organization. Students listen to academic lectures and use provided guidelines to assist with effective note-taking.

In following activities, students participate in a variety of academic listening tasks related to the content of the particular chapter.

Effective Academic Speaking

Activities in this section all resemble types of academic tasks expected of students in the college environment such as taking on roles and participating appropriately in small group formal and informal discussions on lecture content, case studies, or personal experiences, presenting oral summaries, giving short presentations and participating in study groups.

Assessing Your Academic Listening and Speaking Skills

Additional academic listening and speaking and note-taking tasks are provided with similar content material to allow students to demonstrate that they have mastered the objectives of the chapter. In addition, students are given the opportunity to reflect on several of the academic strategies they learned and practiced in the chapter. Each chapter ends with a listing of the chapter objectives for students to evaluate their progress.

Acknowledgments

The good qualities of this book are the result of the excellent advice and help of wonderful colleagues. These include my sage and guide, series co-editor Pat Byrd, my comrade and mentor Linda Robinson Fellag, and the gifted and caring development editor at Houghton Mifflin, Kathy Sands Boehmer. I am grateful to all of them for a chance to learn about learning. I am also indebted to other colleagues at Community College of Philadelphia, particularly Donald Bowers (Behavioral Science), John Braxton (Biology), and Sue Ellen Liebman (History) who were so generous in giving me an entrance into the language of disciplines beyond my own, and to Li-Lee Tunceren and Joy Reid who so patiently helped me think through the teaching of literature. I'm grateful for the unflinching feedback from my colleagues and advisors Elizabeth Cuidet, Jane La Motte, and Robert Simonson. My fellow authors, Marsha Chan, Cheryl Delk, and Ann Roemer were indispensable sources of insight and help.

Reviewers who contributed to the quality of this book include:

Marsha Abramovich of Tidewater Community College
Miranda Joyce Childe of Miami-Dade Community College
Mary Diaz of Broward Community College
Sterling Giles of Roxbury Community College
Mary Goodman of Boca Raton, Florida
Elizabeth Hanley of Community College of Southern Nevada
Meredith Kemper of Florida Community College at Jacksonville
Elaine Matrician of Sussex Community College
Margarita McAuliffe of Palo Alto College
Shirley Terrell of Collin County Community College
Cynthia McKeag-Tsukamoto of Oakton Community College
Shelagh Rose of Pasadena City College
John Sparks of Portland Community College
Mark Tremper of Glendale Community College
Anastassia Tzoytzoyrakos of University of Southern California
Los Angeles, Olivia Villagra of North Lake College
Hoda Zaki of Camden Community College
Kathy Zuo of William Rainey Harper College

I must also acknowledge the help and good humor of so many of my students at Community College of Philadelphia, who added immeasurably to this project by patiently going through the rough spots with me.

The work in this book is dedicated to Marci Resnick, a teacher of teachers, and to the memory of Anna Richardson Jones, 1853–1916.

☐ What Student Competencies Are Covered in *College Oral Communication 4*?

Houghton Mifflin English for Academic Success Competencies
College Oral Communication 4

Description of Overall Purposes:

Students further develop communication skills necessary for full participation in mainstream college classrooms including comprehension of extensive discourse.

With the Materials in This Book, a Student Will Learn:

Production

Competency 1: The student can make her/himself understood by most mainstream listeners in professional and academic situations.

Competency 2: The student will use supra-segmental (e.g., rhythm, stress, intonation) and extra linguistic features to convey precise meaning.

Competency 3: The student will use formal and informal language (persuasion, negotiation, debate, etc.) tailored to specific audiences and contextual settings.

Competency 4: The student will be able to ask questions appropriately during class lectures and discussions so that the student can better understand the content of a lecture/discussion, demonstrate ability to participate in a discussion, and gather information needed for tests and other academic tasks.

Comprehension

Competency 5: The student will be able to comprehend, analyze, synthesize, and summarize extensive discourse.

Competency 6: The student will be able to take notes during academic lectures and to use the notes to prepare for examinations and other academically appropriate uses of notes.

Competency 7: The student will be able to adjust listening strategies according to the complexity and content of the task at hand.

Competency 8: The student will demonstrate the following analytical listening skills:

Distinguish facts/data from generalizations/theory.

Interpret a teacher's purposes, point of view, tone, or use of figurative language in a classroom lecture.

Select the most important information presented during a classroom lecture/discussion to include in notes to prepare for tests and other academic tasks.

☐ What Are the Features of the Oral Communication Books?

The Houghton Mifflin English for Academic Success series is a comprehensive program of student and instructor materials. The fundamental purpose of the program is to prepare students who are not native speakers of English for academic success in U.S. college degree programs.

The Oral Communication strand of the Houghton Mifflin English for Academic Success series focuses on development of speaking and listening skills necessary for college study. Dedicated to meeting academic needs of students by teaching them how to handle the spoken English used by instructors and students in college classrooms, the four books provide engaging activities to practice both academic listening and academic speaking. Students learn to participate effectively in a variety of academic situations, including discussions, lectures, study groups, and office meetings with their college instructors.

Broad Disciplinary Themes: Each book has a broad disciplinary theme to give coherence to the content. These themes were selected because of their high interest for students. They are also topics commonly explored in introductory college courses and so provide useful background for students.

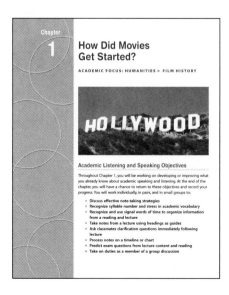

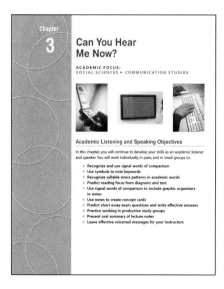

Effective Academic Listening: Students listen to authentic classroom interactions and lectures. They learn to take information from the spoken presentations and use their notes for other academic tasks such as tests or small group discussions.

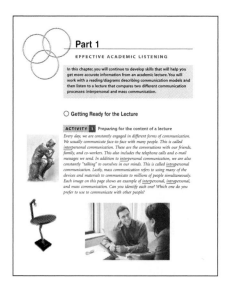

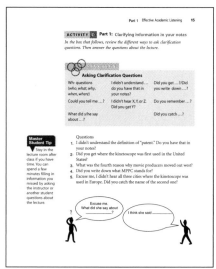

Effective Academic Speaking: Speaking tasks resemble types of academic tasks expected of students in the college environment. These speaking tasks include taking on roles and participating in small group formal and informal discussions on lecture content, presenting oral summaries, to leaving effective voicemail messages. Students learn to do oral presentations appropriate to their proficiency level and to college study.

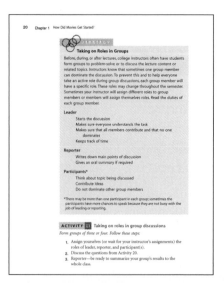

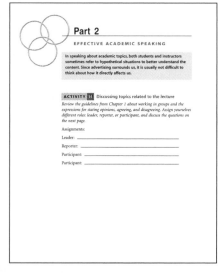

Self-Assessment of Academic Listening and Speaking Skills: Students are given the opportunity to reflect on several of the academic strategies they learned and practiced in the chapters. Each chapter ends with a listing of the chapter objectives for students to evaluate their progress.

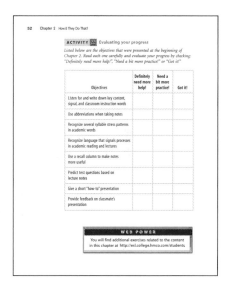

Academic Vocabulary: The Oral Communication strand teaches students techniques for learning and using new academic vocabulary in order to recognize the words when they hear them and to also use the words in their own spoken English.

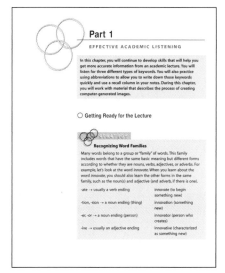

Academic Listening and Speaking Strategies: Key strategies and skills are interspersed throughout each book. Students can clearly see important concepts to focus on as they complete the activities in each chapter. Highlighted strategies will help students improve both their listening and speaking skills.

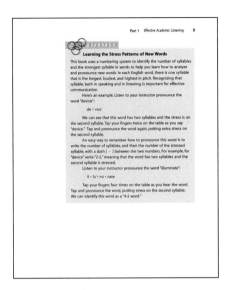

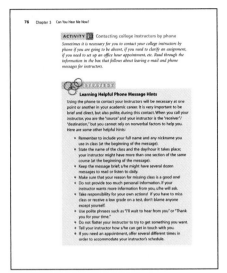

Master Student Tips: Master Student Tips throughout the textbooks provide students with short comments on a particular strategy, activity, or practical advice to follow in an academic setting. Instructors can use these tips to help students become better students by building their understanding of college study.

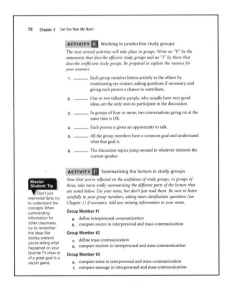

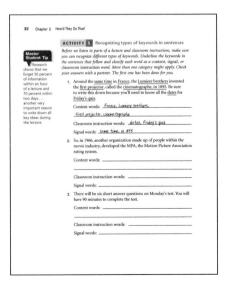

Power Grammar Boxes: Students can be very diverse in their grammar and rhetorical needs so each chapter contains Power Grammar boxes that introduce the grammar structures students need to be fluent and accurate in academic English.

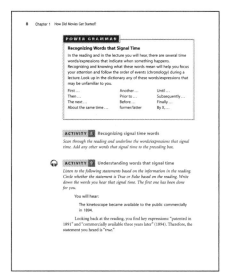

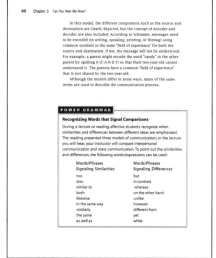

Ancillary Program: The following items are available to accompany the Houghton Mifflin English for Academic Success series Oral Communication strand.

- Instructor website: Additional teaching materials, activities, and robust student assessment.
- Student website: Additional exercises and activities.
- Audio Program: Available on either CD-ROM or cassette.
- The Houghton Mifflin English for Academic Success Series Vocabulary books: You can choose the appropriate level to shrinkwrap with your text.
- *The Essentials of Teaching Academic Oral Communication* by John Murphy is available for purchase. It gives you theoretical and practical information for teaching oral communication.

Chapter 1

Money, Power, and Everyday Life in the Ancient World

ACADEMIC FOCUS: HISTORY

Academic Listening and Speaking Objectives

In this textbook you will study the language used by instructors and students in college classes. Many times college instructors give lectures, that is, they talk to the whole class in a formal way, and explain material from the course.

In this chapter, you will learn some of the language skills students need to do well in a history course. In part of the chapter, you will learn about listening to a formal lecture. In another part, you will learn about working with classmates to summarize part of a lecture, and you will work with written material on the same topic. The topic of the lecture is the development of money in ancient society. Objectives:

- ▓ **Recognize syllable stress in academic vocabulary**
- ▓ **Learn the meanings of academic vocabulary**
- ▓ **Recognize advanced time expressions**
- ▓ **Take notes on important points in a lecture**
- ▓ **Work as a member of a group on an academic task**
- ▓ **Summarize the main points of a lecture**

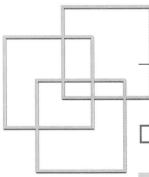

Part 1

☐ Getting Ready for Academic Listening

ACTIVITY 1 Discussing the content of a lecture

Part 1

To understand the lecture, The Development of Money in the Ancient World, you will need to have some basic background knowledge about the ancient world. Below are some place names that you will hear in the lecture. Work with a partner. Find these places on the map below, [Map 1], which shows the location of places in the Mediterranean and part of the Middle East in ancient times. Your instructor will help you with the English pronunciation of unfamiliar words. Have you studied or heard about any of these places before? What do you know about them?

Greece	Aegina[4]
Mesopotamia	Lydia
Nippur[1]	Ionia
Canaan[2]	Persia
Mycenae[3]	Athens

1. ni pŏŏr´
2. kā´ nən
3. mī sē´ nē
4. ə jē´ nə

Part 2

The following questions are about the history of money. Most of them will be answered in the lecture. Although you may not yet know the answers, discuss the questions with your partner, and write down your answers. After you finish, put your answers aside. You will use them later.

1. The timeline shows some important events in human history. Study the timeline and think about this question: How old is money? In other words, where does it fit on this timeline?

Human civilization (Years BCE–CE)

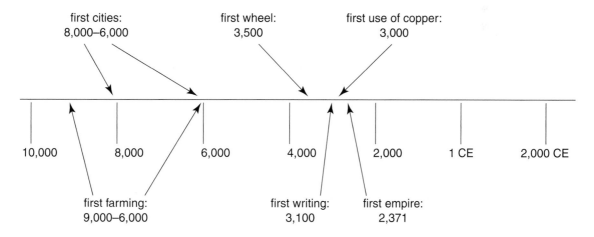

2. In what part of the world did money first develop?
3. In what order did people develop the following:
   a. trade
   b. money
   c. accounting
4. When people invented money, how did society change?
   a. Did society become more developed or less developed?
   b. Did society become more peaceful or less peaceful?
   c. Did people become more equal or less equal?
5. What did the first money look like?
   a. What was it made of?
   b. What shape was it?
   c. What kinds of images or pictures were on it?

☐ Learning New Academic Vocabulary

In this textbook you will learn about special vocabulary that is used in college-level, or academic, situations. This vocabulary is from a list called the Academic Word List (AWL). The AWL is a set of 570 groups of related words that have been found in examples of writing in many different college subjects. The words on the list are not common ones that you will meet in everyday life. The AWL words are also not words found in only one or two academic subjects. When you learn about AWL words, you are learning about the words that will be most helpful to you in understanding lectures or readings in a variety of college classes. In this book, you will focus on studying the pronunciation and meaning of many of the AWL words.

When you work with vocabulary in this book, you should make a list of words that are new to you, and make a special effort to learn those words. Some activities are designed to help you find out which words you already know well, and which words you need to learn.

☐ Learning the Stress Pattern of Academic Vocabulary

This book uses a system for writing some of the details about the pronunciation of new words, so that you can recognize them when you hear them and can pronounce them accurately when you need to say them. These details include the number of syllables in the word and the syllable that receives the strongest, or primary, stress. In each English word there is one syllable that is longest, loudest, and highest in pitch. Recognizing that syllable, both in speaking and in listening, is important for effective communication.

For each new word, or for each new form of a word, that you learn in this book, you should also learn the number of syllables it has and the number of the stressed syllable. Knowing these will improve your ability to recognize academic words that you may have seen only in writing.

An example is the word "item" in this chapter. This word has two syllables. (Your instructor can help you count syllables if this is difficult for you.) The stressed syllable in "item" is the first syllable. We use a simple system to note these two facts about a word. We write the number of syllables, and then the number of the stressed syllable, with a dash (-) between the two numbers. For example, for "item" we would write [2-1], meaning that the word has two syllables and the stress is on the first syllable. For "evolve" we would write [2-2], meaning that the word has two syllables and the stress is on the second syllable.

ACTIVITY 2   Analyzing syllable-stress

Use the notation system to help you pronounce these words correctly. Your instructor will help you. Here is an example:

de • vel • op [__3__ - __2__]

This means that "develop" has three syllables and the stress is on the second syllable. This information should help you pronounce "develop" correctly.

1. achievement [__3__ - __2__]

2. area [__3__ - __1__]

3. commodity [__4__ - __2__]

4. creation [__3__ - __2__]

5. dominant [__3__ - __1__]

6. economic [__4__ - __3__]

7. evolved [__2__ - __2__]

8. guarantee [__3__ - __3__]

9. period [__3__ - __1__]

10. purchases [__3__ - __1__]

ACTIVITY 3   **Practicing word pronunciation**

Listen to your instructor pronounce these words. Use the notation system to record the number of syllables and the stressed syllable. The first two are done for you. When you are finished, review your answers with your instructor.

1. maintain   [_2_ - _2_]

2. ranging   [_2_ - _1_]

3. secure   [__ - __]

4. security   [__ - __]

5. specific   [__ - __]

6. stylized   [__ - __]

7. symbolized   [__ - __]

8. transaction   [__ - __]

ACTIVITY 4 Working with academic vocabulary

First, review the list of words that follow, and put a check by those that you know well. For the words whose meanings you know, match each word with the letter of the meaning that is closest to the word's meaning. For words whose meaning you do not know, get help from your dictionary, a classmate, or your instructor. When you are finished, review your answers with your class. Use the answers to keep your own list of words you need to study. The first one is done as an example.

1. achievement _K_

2. area ____

3. commodity ____

4. creation ____

5. dominant ____

6. economic ____

7. evolved ____

8. guarantee ____

9. period ____

10. purchases ____

11. ranging ____

12. maintain ____

13. secure ____

14. security ____

15. specific ____

16. stylized ____

17. symbolized ____

18. transaction ____

Meanings:
   a. developed; changed
   b. going from one value or number to another
   c. something that people buy and sell
   d. most important or strongest
   e. an act of buying and selling
   f. amount of time
   g. related to making and exchanging things that are valuable
   h. safety
   i. promise
   j. place; part of the world
   k. accomplishment; something important that someone was able to do
   l. not general; particular
   m. changed so that something does not have all its details
   n. things that people buy
   o. safe
   p. showed the meaning of something
   q. something that someone made
   r. keep

S T R A T E G Y

Using a Text to Prepare for Academic Listening

Instructors use some of the vocabulary and ideas from a textbook in their lectures. If you work to recognize those words and ideas in writing, it can be easier to understand them when you hear them in a lecture.

This vase, made in Athens in about 500 BCE, shows merchants making up containers of equal weight.

☐ Using the Text to Prepare for Academic Listening

Successful students often use a reading passage to help them prepare for lecture material. Instructors use some of the vocabulary and ideas from a textbook in their lectures. If you read your textbook before a lecture, it is easier to recognize and understand those words in the lecture.

ACTIVITY 5   **Using your textbook to prepare for a lecture**

Read the following passage from a history textbook. Take notes about important ideas in the passage, and use a dictionary to find out the meaning of words that interest you. (You do not need to know many of the unusual words used in this passage.) A table related to the same topic follows the reading.

THE ECONOMIES OF THE GREEK WORLD

1 The first currencies all over the ancient world were pieces of precious metal with no fixed value: copper, bronze, silver, and infrequently gold. The only way to evaluate such a piece of metal was to weigh it using a standard set of weights; in time, merchants began to guarantee the purity of the bullion[1] they used by stamping a recognizable device[2] on each unit. The earliest examples of such private coinage come from Ionia. We are told that in mainland Greece, in the archaic period, minor exchanges were negotiated by means of obols or spits of metal, iron, or bronze, and that six obols equaled a drachma—literally, a "handful"—derived from the Greek verb meaning to grasp. But until the first half of the sixth century BC, the Greeks lived in a largely premonetary society, relying on barter[3] to obtain items they could not grow or make themselves.

The Development of Coinage

2 The kingdom of Lydia was the first state to guarantee both the weight and purity of pieces of metal by turning out standardized currency marked with the symbol of the realm.[4] By the late seventh century, Ionian Greek neighbors had adopted this custom, and it quickly spread to the islands and to mainland Greece, particularly to the highly commercialized island of Aegina, just south of Athens.

3 From the evidence of large coin hoards,[5] it would seem that Aegina, Corinth, and Chalcis (on the island of Euboea) dominated Aegean trade until the first part of the fifth century. Sometime in the middle of the sixth century BC, the Athenians adopted the coinage standard of Chalsis, which was gaining wide acceptance in Aegean trading.

1. *bullion* = pure metal such as silver, gold, etc.
2. *device* = a symbol
3. *barter* = trading one good for another good
4. *realm* = country
5. *hoards* = very large collections of coins that were found in one place

4   Athenian coinage can serve as a model for the currencies of other Greek cities issued in more or less the same denominations.[6] The smallest coin was a tiny bit of silver (or a larger slug of copper or bronze) worth one-eighth of an obol. Larger divisions of the obol were one-quarter, three-eighths, one-half, and three-quarters. Six obols equaled one drachma, one hundred drachmas made a mina, and sixty minas, a talent. The major denomination for larger transactions was the tetra-drachm, or *stater.*

5   It is almost impossible to equate Attic[7] or other Greek money with modern currency. The only way to approximate the Athenian standard of wages and prices is to compare the average daily wage of the working person against prices of food, clothing, and other commodities.

6   By the last decade of the fifth century,[8] no doubt due to war-caused inflation, the daily wage of a laborer had gone up to one drachma, and it is against this standard that we must measure prices. If we assume the Athenian laborer's daily wage during Socrates' day to have been one drachma and his modern American counterpart's to be about $100.00 (average, after taxes and other deductions), we see immediately that by our standards, the city was by no means cheap. A quart of olives by this equation would cost about $2.08 and eight quarts of barley meal $16.67—reasonable enough—but the tunic, a simple woolen sleeveless garment worn by the poor, would cost $1,000.00!

7   We can compare the range of prices at this time by looking at the accompanying table (see page 12). As can be seen, Athenian prices bear little relationship to present-day U.S. prices. The cost of a few things like furniture and livestock may be more or less equivalent, but any American would find food prices (with the exception of figs, olives, and other staples), as well as the cost of the simplest kinds of garments and shoes, wildly exorbitant.[9]

---

6. *denominations* = the value of coins or bills such as five cents, ten dollars, etc.
7. *Attic* = of ancient Athens
8. *the last decade of the fifth century* = the ten years after 410 BCE
9. *exorbitant* = very high in price

8   But one must always bear in mind that the Athenian style of life was entirely different from that of twentieth-century America. Very few Athenians had large, fixed, monthly expenses like rent, and of course none of them had utility bills, insurance, car payments and so forth. A large part of the diet of every working class Greek was barley boiled up into porridge or made into barley cake, and one could buy a quart (enough to glut[10] a family of five for a whole day) for one copper, that is, one-eighth obol or about $2.08 by our scale. A loaf of bread also lasted a day for the same family, and although the price to us seems absurdly high, we must remember that the Athenian family was accustomed to eating very little else: some garlic or onions and cheese to flavor the bread or porridge, beans and other legumes, figs and olives, on occasion a little fish, octopus, or meat. Furthermore, one must remember that not all food had to be bought. Almost everyone tried to maintain a kitchen garden and a few sheep or goats for milk and cheese. Gray mullet, anchovies, and octopus[11] were free to anyone who could lay his hands on a net or a barbed spear.[12]

9   Cloaks, tunics,[13] and shoes seem very expensive when measured against daily income. But the average Athenian generally possessed only one set of garments and one pair of shoes; this wardrobe was made to last a lifetime, with repairs. Once again, most Athenian families would not have had to pay the full retail price given in the accompanying table, because there were usually females present who could card, spin, and weave wool.

10   Our sources show that Athenian life was quite frugal.[14] There was an upper stratum of great wealth: we read of families being able to pay 50-talent fines, estates valued at 80 and 100 talents, women buying 1,000-drachma dresses, and young men spending fortunes on horses. But for the most part, even the rich lived modestly, wore simple clothes, and built houses not much more elegant than those of the poorest citizens.

Frank J. Frost, *Greek Society*, Fifth Edition. Copyright © 1997 by Houghton Mifflin Company. Reprinted with permission.

10. *glut* = completely fill up
11. *gray mullet, anchovies, and octopus* = sea life that can be eaten
12. *barbed spear* = a long, sharp tool used for catching animals by stabbing them
13. *cloaks, tunics* = ancient forms of clothing similar to a coat and a shirt
14. *frugal* = living in a way to keep expenses low

Prices of commodities in ancient Athens		
Commodity:	**Cost (in coppers):**	**Cost in modern dollars:**
a loaf of bread	8	17
barley for a whole day's meals	1	2
a salted fish	8	17
shoes	336	700
cloak	480	1,000
dream interpretation	12	25
cosmetics	16	33
sheep	576	1,200
Thracian slave	7,200	15,000
Syrian slave	12,000	25,000

ACTIVITY **6** **Getting content from a reading**

Write answers to these questions about the reading. Be prepared to discuss your answers with your class.

1. In ancient times, how did people find out the value of metal pieces that were used in trade?
2. How did ancient merchants know that the metal in money was pure?
3. What states were the first to use money?
4. What things were expensive for the ancient Athenians, compared to today? What things were inexpensive?
5. How did Athenians cope with the high prices of many goods?

☐ Getting Information from a Lecture

When you listen to a class lecture in a history course, you often need to:

- take notes while the instructor is talking; your notes will help you remember what the instructor said
- take notes about course assignments
- take notes about the date of tests, and the material you will be tested on
- help yourself, the other students, and the instructor by answering or asking questions about the material during the lecture

In this chapter, you will take notes about what the lecturer says about the development of money.

One important part of listening to a lecture in an academic class is selecting important information from all the words that you hear. Successful students are able to select this important information and write it in a way that helps them remember it later. Recording this important information is called *taking notes*.

One of the challenges of note-taking is that speaking is much faster than writing. Since your instructor can talk faster than you can write, it is not possible to write exactly what you hear. Here are three specific tips to make taking notes easier and faster for you:

1. Mainly use content words (main verbs, nouns, adjectives, and adverbs) in your notes.

   You may sometimes also wish to use prepositions (such as *to*, *in*, *at*). Writing fewer words will allow you to write faster, and you will still be able to understand your notes later.

   Example: In the lecture for this chapter, you will hear the sentence:

   Trading metal was a step in the development of money.

   In your notes, using only content words and prepositions, you might write:

   Trading metal step in development of money.

   if you want to remember this idea.

2. Write abbreviations for long words.

   The words *society* and *economic* are used in the lecture, and you may choose to write them in your notes. It is faster to write abbreviations for academic words like these, including any forms the word has. For example, *society, social, socially* can be abbreviated as *soc.* and *economic, economy, economical* can be abbreviated as *ec.* In the sentence:

   > Money met some of the economic needs of society.

   you could write,

   > Money met ec. needs of soc.

   In the first example, you could use an abbreviation for "development" and write:

   > Trading metal step in dev of money

3. Make your own set of easy symbols for words that are used very often.

   Successful students often use short symbols for very common words. Examples are *w/* for *with* or @ for *at.* Sometimes a word is very common in a particular subject or lecture, and it saves time to shorten the way to write it. For example, in this chapter's lecture, the word *trade* occurs many times. To save time, you can use *tr.* as a symbol for *trade* and related words. If the speaker says:

   > People all over the world traded with each other.

   You might write:

   > People all over world tr. w/ e.o.

   Another example is using "$" for "money," a word that appears many times in the lecture.

   Now the sentence:

   > Trading metal was a step in development of money.

   could be:

   > Tr metal step in dev of $.

ACTIVITY 7 Taking notes from a lecture

Your instructor will give you some examples of sentences that you will hear in a lecture in this chapter. As you listen, take notes. Write only the important words, and use abbreviations for common words. When you finish, discuss your answers with your class. Your classmates might have good ideas for abbreviations you can use.

Example: Pieces of metal did not have standard weights, so merchants had to weigh them.

Notes: *Pieces of metal: no std. wts, so merch weigh*

1.

2.

3.

4.

5.

POWER GRAMMAR

Time Expressions

In the lecture you will hear, much of the information is about time. The speaker tells when important events happened, and also the relationship between important events. If you understand a few important expressions about time, the lecture will be easier for you.

1. **Time expression: years BCE and CE.** The events in this lecture cover a period of about 5,000 years. It is very important to understand the time in history that is being discussed. The lecturer often tells the year that important changes occurred with the word *in* and a year. In this lecture, the speaker uses the term *BCE* to refer to the years before the commonly used Year 1. *BCE* stands for "before the common era." The phrase "1,000 BCE" means the time about three thousand years ago. The speaker also uses the term *CE* to refer to years after the commonly accepted Year 1. *CE* refers to "common era." The phrase "1,000 CE" means the time about one thousand years ago. Other speakers or other books may use the terms *BC* ("before Christ') or *AD* (anno Domini) instead of *BCE* and *CE*. Here is an example:

   Archeologists have found jars of pure metal pieces in jars made in Canaan **in about 1,000 BCE.**

   It is important to hear the number and BCE after *in*. This tells us that the metal pieces were made about three thousand years ago, a thousand years before the "common era," which is a little more than two thousand years old.

2. **Time expression: "the first _____."** Often the lecture speaker tells about the beginnings of changes. Often, these changes are explained with *the first _____*, as in these examples:

   The first true money was in the form of coins, which were pieces of pure metal with a known weight.

   Some of **the first money** we know about was made near the Mediterranean Sea.

(Continued)

3. **Time expressions:**
   after _____
   before _____

   Some of the information in the lecture is about the order of events. That is, the speaker tells us which things happened first. In many cases, the speaker shows this relationship by using *after* or *before*. Sometimes these words are followed by a noun phrase, and sometimes by a clause. (If you are not sure what a *noun phrase* or a *clause* is, you may want to review this with your instructor, or you may want to check a grammar book.) Here are examples:

   > **Before the invention of money**, people all over the world traded with each other.

   > **After the invention of money** in the ancient world, states competed to have their money accepted most widely.

   > **After the Greeks lost their empire around 31 BCE**, the Romans became the economic leaders of a big part of the Mediterranean area.

ACTIVITY **8**   **Listening for time expressions**

Your instructor will give you some examples of sentences that use time expressions. As you listen, take notes. Use abbreviations, as the example shows. When you finish, discuss your answers with your class.

For example, if you hear:

Other early money was made in Persia, around 500 BCE.

You can write:

Early $ in Persia, abt 500 BCE

1.

2.

3.

4.

5.

☐ Using Graphic Information for Academic Listening

ACTIVITY 9 **Getting information from illustrations**

Work with a partner. Study the map on page 2 and the timeline on page 3. The timeline shows important events in the development of money. The map and the timeline are illustrations that will help make the lecture more clear. With your partner, review the information on the map and the timeline. Your instructor will ask you to report what you discussed.

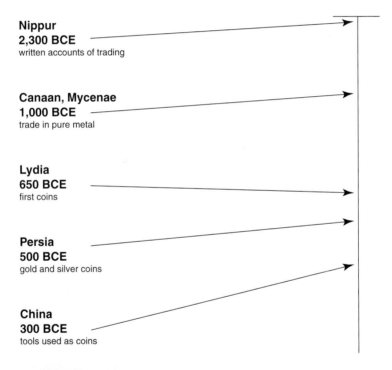

Nippur
2,300 BCE
written accounts of trading

Canaan, Mycenae
1,000 BCE
trade in pure metal

Lydia
650 BCE
first coins

Persia
500 BCE
gold and silver coins

China
300 BCE
tools used as coins

This is one of the first coins used in world trade, the Athenian *drachma*. It shows a picture of the goddess Athena.

ACTIVITY 10   **Listening to a lecture and taking notes**

Now you will listen to a lecture and take notes that will help you remember what you heard. Below is a list of important questions about the lecture. If you understand the answers to these questions, you will understand the lecture's main points. Together, the questions make an outline of the lecture.

Review the questions with your class before you listen. Make sure you understand the questions, even if you do not know the answers. Then, while listening, try to write answers to the questions. Use the note-taking skills you practiced in Activity 7 and Activity 8.

Here is an example. In the lecture, you will hear this:

> The development of money is one of the big achievements of the ancient world. It helped increase the ability of people to trade products over long distances, and it helped the creation of wealthy empires.

The first part of the outline for the lecture looks like this:

Part 1. Money in ancient society

How did money change the ancient world?

_____

_____

When you write notes on this section, think about the answer to the question "How did money change the ancient world?" A good set of notes would look like this:

> incr ability tr over long dist
> helped create emps

The outline is divided into eight parts or sections. Your instructor will decide how many parts of the lecture to work with before you stop to review your notes. Your instructor may repeat all or part of the lecture before you move to the activity. When you finish this activity, you will have a good set of notes about the lecture.

Part 1. Money in ancient society

How did money change the ancient world?

_____

_____

How old is money?

_____

_____

Where did money first develop?

_____

Part 2. Trade and money

Before the invention of money, what were examples of goods and products that ancient societies traded?

_____

_____

_____

_____

Which is older, accounting or money?

_____

_____

Part 3. Needs of ancient society

What are some economic needs that ancient society had?

_____

_____

_____

Part 4. Problems in trading without money

What are examples of ancient societies that used metal in trade?

_____

_____

_____

What problems did ancient merchants have with using metal as a commodity?

_____

_____

Part 5. Money as a solution

What was the form of the first money? What special qualities did early money have?

_____

_____

_____

_____

How did money solve the problems of standardization and purity?

_____

_____

_____

What economic needs did money meet?

_____

_____

_____

_____

_____

Part 6. The first money societies

How did states guarantee that coins had a certain weight and purity?

_____

_____

What are examples of societies that made early money? When did they first use money?

_____

_____

_____

_____

Part 7. International competition

Which states had a better chance to have their money accepted by other societies?

_____

_____

_____

_____

Why was Athens important in the development of money?

_____

What did Athenians use money for?

_____

What society followed the Greeks in making popular forms of money?

_____

Part 8. How money changed the world

How did money change the ancient economic world?

_____

_____

_____

ACTIVITY 11   Reviewing lecture notes

Work with a partner and review the notes you made on the outline in Activity 10. Discuss what you wrote. You may want to make changes in your notes after you discuss them with your partner. Also, review this chapter's textbook reading. Look for information in the reading that can help answer the questions in the outline. When you finish, review your answers to the questions in the outline with your instructor and your class.

ACTIVITY 12   Answering questions about a lecture

Review your answers to the questions in Activity 1, Part 2, on page 3. Do you have better answers to these questions now? These are some possible answers:

How old is money?

> The first money was made in about 650 BCE, and it became popular in many places around 500 BCE, so money is about 2,500 years old.

In what part of the world did money first develop?

> Rulers in Lydia and Ionia made the first money. Lydia and Ionia were between Europe and Asia, near the Mediterranean.

In what order did people develop these things: trade, money, accounting?

> Trade came first, then accounting (in Mesopotamia), then money.

When people invented money, how did society change?

> Money made it possible to do business on a much bigger scale, and it made the development of military empires more possible.

What did the first money look like? What was it made of? What shape was it? What kinds of images or pictures were on it?

> The first money was a standard size piece of pure metal with a picture on it.

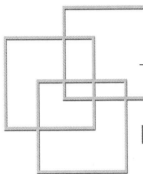

Part 2

EFFECTIVE ACADEMIC SPEAKING

☐ Roles for Working in Groups

College instructors often require students to work in groups to carry out projects. To be successful in college, you need strategies to be an effective group member and to help your group do its work well.

In this textbook, you will sometimes speak as a member of a small group. As a group member, you will always have a specific job, called a *role*. You should learn how to work in each role that is used in this textbook. The roles are:

Leader

This person leads the group in the job or task they are asked to do. The leader makes sure that all group members understand the assignment. The leader also tries to make sure that the job gets finished and that all group members get a chance to speak. This may mean encouraging quieter members by asking them questions or helping them in other ways.

Reporter

In each group speaking assignment, there is always a decision or a result of the group's discussion. The group is always asked to report to the entire class the result of their discussion. The reporter's job is to take notes on what group members say, and to give a summary to the larger group (that is, the whole class) about the discussion or other work of the smaller group.

Participant

Group members who are not leaders or reporters still have very important jobs. They are to think about the discussion topic, and participate in the group's work. Sometimes participants have more chances to speak because they are not busy leading or reporting. There may be more than one participant in each group.

You will get a chance to fill one of the roles in the speaking assignment that follows. Your instructor will ask you to take one of the roles.

ACTIVITY 13   **Preparing a lecture summary**

Students often study together in college classes. They sometimes meet outside of class to review their notes and to help each other understand what is discussed in class.

In this activity, you will work in a small group to prepare a summary of the lecture on the history of money. Form a group of three to five students, and use the roles that are described above.

Begin by writing a set of notes that will help the reporter remember the important points in the summary. (The leader will organize the group to do the task; the reporter will write the notes and give a summary to the whole class.) Use your notes, the map, and the timeline to help with this activity. Your instructor may ask you to prepare your summary for the whole lecture, or for only some of its eight parts.

When you make an oral summary, your notes are a good place to start. Find the most important points in your notes, and give an explanation or example about each point.

Here is an example. Your notes for Part 4 of the lecture might say:

Probs w/ trade in metal:

No standard weights, merch. had to weigh

Merch had to carry scales, weights

Your oral summary could be:

There were some problems with trading pieces of metal. One problem was that there were no standard weights, so merchants had to weigh the metal every time they traded it. They had to carry scales and weights with them when they traded.

ACTIVITY 14 Analyzing a chart

The chart on page 12 shows the cost of some goods in ancient Athens, which was the first society to use money for daily transactions. In this society, an average worker earned about one drachma *per day, which was worth six* obols. *The smallest Athenian coin was a* copper, *which was worth one-eighth of an obol. This means that an average worker would earn about forty-eight coppers per day.*

The prices on the list are in coppers. The list also shows approximately how much the goods would cost in modern U.S. dollars, if we assume that a worker earns $100 a day.

Use the roles for working in groups. Discuss these questions:

1. What things on this list are surprising to you? For example, are some of the costs surprising?
2. Did the average worker earn enough to buy food? How do you know?
3. What do you notice about the cost of clothes? What conclusion can you make from this?
4. Could the average person afford a slave to work for them?
5. What does the presence of "dream interpretation" tell us about Greek life and thinking?
6. Ancient Greek society was one of the first in which people earned money in exchange for work. What changes in society would happen because of this change?

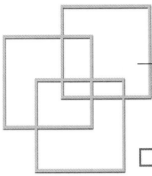

Part 3

ASSESSING YOUR ACADEMIC LISTENING AND SPEAKING SKILLS

☐ Listening to a Short Lecture

 ACTIVITY 15 Listening to a lecture and taking notes

Listen to the short lecture that follows. While listening, take notes on the important points.

Look at the following "blackboard notes" while you listen. These notes show what the history instructor writes on a blackboard to help students during class. The blackboard notes will help you follow the lecture's content. You can add information to them to make your own set of notes.

Your instructor will give you some written questions to answer about this lecture. Use your notes to answer the questions.

History of <u>dollar</u>:

After end of the Greek dominance:
    Arab dinar
Roman denarius
    Spain: money first made 1000 CE.
United Spanish kingdom 1479:
    Colonies in the Western Hemisphere
Spanish coin: eight reales
    English-speaking colonies
        former English colonies with dollars:
            United States, Jamaica, Australia, Canada

ACTIVITY 16 Preparing a short oral summary

In this activity you will work on your own. Imagine a classmate asked you for a summary of the short lecture in Activity 13. Review your notes. Prepare to summarize the talk. Your instructor might ask you to give your oral summary to a small group or to the whole class.

When you make an oral summary, start by reviewing your notes. Find the most important points in your notes, and make sure you give an explanation or example about each. For example, the blackboard notes from the lecture in Activity 13 include this note:

After end of Greek dominance, new countries made coins
    Roman denarius
    Arab dinar

When you summarize this part of the lecture, you might say:

> After the period of Greek dominance ended, new countries made their own coins. For example, Romans made a coin called the denarius and Arab rulers made a coin called the dinar.

If possible, use words from the Academic Word List in your summary. Use this list to review the pronunciation and meaning of the vocabulary words from this chapter:

1. achievement		**10.** purchases
2. area		**11.** ranging
3. commodity		**12.** maintain
4. creation		**13.** secure
5. dominant		**14.** security
6. economic		**15.** specific
7. evolved		**16.** stylized
8. guarantee		**17.** symbolized
9. period		**18.** transaction

☐ Assessing Your Speaking

ACTIVITY 17 Getting feedback on your speaking skills

Your instructor may use this checklist to let you know about your use of academic English in your speaking assignments.

Summary of the lecture	OK	Needs work	Example(s)
Content:			
▪ accurately summarized content of the lecture			
Organization:			
▪ explained time order of events			
Vocabulary:			
▪ used stress appropriately in academic vocabulary			
Speaking grammar:			
▪ used time expressions correctly			

☐ Self-Assessment

ACTIVITY 18 Evaluating your progress

Review this list of chapter objectives. Think about your work and progress in each of these areas. Make a mark after objectives that need your special attention in future work on academic speaking and listening.

- Recognize syllable stress in academic vocabulary _____

- Learn the meanings of academic vocabulary _____

- Recognize advanced time expressions _____

- Take notes on important points in a lecture _____

- Work as a group member of a group on an academic task _____

- Summarize the main points of a lecture _____

Look back at this list after you finish the work in the next chapter.

WEB POWER

You will find additional exercises related to the content in this chapter at http://esl.college.hmco.com/students.

2

Is Big Business Controlling Your Mind?

ACADEMIC FOCUS: PSYCHOLOGY

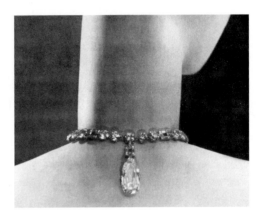

Academic Listening and Speaking Objectives

In this chapter, you will practice skills to help you obtain information from a formal lecture. You will learn how to use this information to do academic assignments, including participating in class by asking questions, working in a study group to prepare for a test, and taking tests.

You will work with material about the connection between *psychology* and *advertising*. Psychology is the study of human behavior. Advertising is a business activity that affects consumer behavior. Objectives are to:

- Learn the stress pattern and meaning of new academic vocabulary
- Recognize and take notes on cause and effect expressions
- Recognize and understand past participles used as adjectives
- Take notes on a lecture's main points and details
- Compare and clarify lecture notes with classmates
- Speak with cause and effect expressions
- Summarize a lecture's important points
- Ask questions for clarification during a lecture
- Prepare for a lecture test
- Prepare a short oral summary

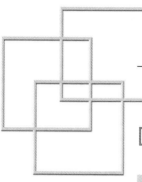

Part 1

☐ **Getting Ready for Academic Listening**

ACTIVITY 1 Discussing the content of a lecture

In this chapter, you will listen to formal lectures about psychology and advertising. To prepare to understand the information in these lectures, discuss these questions in a small group. (Use the roles for group work that you learned about in Chapter 1, page 25). When you finish, your group's reporter will share your answers with the class.

1. What is your favorite advertisement? Where did you see it? What product does it advertise? Why do you like the ad?
2. Study the advertisements that follow. Answer these questions:
   a. What products are the ads selling?
   b. What feelings do these ads seem to connect to? Are the feelings in the ads positive, like security? Are they negative, like fear? Are they neutral?
   c. Who seems to be the audience for these advertisements? What do you think is the age, gender, and income of the people to whom the ad is directed?

Superior Jewelry

. . . one of the good things in life

Beneficial Insurance:

You know what's important

ACTIVITY 2 Analyzing the stress pattern of new vocabulary

The following words are important in the lecture you will hear. Some of them may be new to you. Place a check mark next to the words that you know well. Find the words that are new to you in your dictionary. Be prepared to pronounce all of the words correctly. Use the system for noting the number of syllables and the stressed syllables that you learned in Chapter 1, page 4. (Record the numbers within the brackets that look like this: [___ - ___]. The first two are done for you.) Your instructor may ask you to pronounce these words before you hear the lecture.

1. affect (v.)   [_2_ - _2_]   11. link (v.)   [___ - ___]
2. associate   [_4_ - _2_]   12. neutral   [___ - ___]
3. conditioned   [___ - ___]   13. obvious   [___ - ___]
4. consumer   [___ - ___]   14. pair (v.)   [___ - ___]
5. design (v.)   [___ - ___]   15. physiologist   [___ - ___]
6. digestive   [___ - ___]   16. psychologist [___ - ___]
7. elicit   [___ - ___]   17. research (v.) [___ - ___]
8. emotional   [___ - ___]   18. response   [___ - ___]
9. hypothesis   [___ - ___]   19. stimulus   [___ - ___]
10. image   [___ - ___]   20. unconditioned [___ - ___]

ACTIVITY 3 Learning new academic vocabulary

Learn the meanings of the academic words that are used in this chapter. First, match each of the following words with the phrase that is closest to the word's meaning. Then review your answers with your class. For words you do not know, get help from your dictionary or your instructor. Use the answers for this activity to study the meanings.

1. affect	_____	11. link (v.)	_____
2. associate	_____	12. neutral	_____
3. conditioned	_____	13. obvious	_____
4. consumer	_____	14. physiologist	_____
5. design (v.)	_____	15. pair (v.)	_____
6. digestive	_____	16. psychologist	_____
7. elicit	_____	17. research (v.)	_____
8. emotional	_____	18. response	_____
9. hypothesis	_____	19. stimulus	_____
10. image	_____	20. unconditioned	_____

Meanings:

a. not positive and not negative
b. picture or idea
c. cause something to change
d. study in a careful way
e. prepared to have a specific reaction
f. produce; bring out
g. not needing to be taught; natural
h. related to making use of food in an animal's body
i. a person who is trained to understand human behavior
j. clear; not needing an explanation
k. make a plan
l. put two things together
m. connect, especially in thinking
n. person who buys things
o. something that causes a reaction
p. an idea that might explain why something happens
q. related to feelings
r. reaction; result
s. a person who studies the bodies of animals
t. join together

ACTIVITY 4 **Using your text to prepare for a lecture**

Read the following passage from a psychology textbook. Take notes about important ideas in the passage, and use a dictionary to find out the meaning of words that interest you.

CLASSICAL CONDITIONING: LEARNING SIGNALS AND ASSOCIATIONS

How Did Russian Dogs Teach Psychologists about Learning?

1   At the first notes of the national anthem, a young athlete's heart may begin to pound. Those sounds signal that the game is about to begin. Similarly, a low-fuel light on your car's instrument panel might make your adrenaline[1] flow, because it means that you are almost out of gas. People are not born with these reactions. They have learned them from associations between events in the world. The experimental study of this kind of learning was begun, almost by accident, by Ivan Petrovich Pavlov.

Pavlov's Discovery

2   Although Pavlov is one of the best-known figures in psychology, he was not a psychologist. He was a Russian physiologist who won the Nobel Prize in 1904 for his research on the digestive system of dogs. In the course of this research, Pavlov noticed a strange phenomenon.[2] His dogs sometimes salivated[3] when no food was present. For instance, they salivated when they saw the assistant who normally brought their food.

3   Pavlov devised a simple experiment to determine how salivation could occur without an obvious physical cause, such as food. First he performed an operation to divert a dog's saliva into a container, allowing him to measure precisely how much was secreted. Next he placed the dog in an apparatus[4] similar to the one shown in the figure.

1. *adrenaline* = a chemical produced by the body which causes rapid heart beat and other sudden changes
2. *phenomenon* = something that happens, often as part of a pattern
3. *salivated* = produced a liquid from the mouth that helps in digestion
4. *apparatus* = a piece of equipment

4   The experiment had three phases. In the first phase, Pavlov and his associates confirmed that when meat powder was placed on the dog's tongue, the dog automatically salivated (Anrep, 1920). They also confirmed that the dog did not automatically salivate in response to neutral stimuli, such as a white lab coat or a tone. The researchers thus established the existence of the two basic components for Pavlov's experiment: (1) a natural reflex (in this case, automatic salivation to meat powder placed on the dog's tongue) and (2) a neutral stimulus (the sound of a tone, which by itself would cause no salivation. A *reflex* is the swift, automatic response to a stimulus, such as shivering in the cold or jumping when you are jabbed with a needle. A neutral stimulus is one that does not elicit the reflex being studied.

5   In the second phase of Pavlov's experiment, the tone sounded, and meat powder was placed in the dog's mouth. The dog salivated. This *pairing* of the tone followed by the meat powder was repeated several times. Then, in the third phase, the tone was sounded and no meat powder was presented. The dog again salivated. The tone by itself now made the dog salivate. The tone had come to predict the presentation of the meat powder. You may have seen the same principle in action when you open a can of pet food with an electric can opener. The sound of the can opener may bring your pet running. It means that food is coming.

6   Pavlov's experiment demonstrated what we now call **classical conditioning**. In this procedure, a neutral stimulus is repeatedly paired with a stimulus that already triggers[5] a reflexive response, until the previously neutral stimulus alone provokes a similar response. The stimulus that naturally elicits a response *without* conditioning, such as the meat powder in Pavlov's experiment, is called the **unconditioned stimulus (UCS)**. The automatic, unlearned, reflexive response to this stimulus is called the **unconditioned response (UCR)**. The neutral stimulus (tone), after being paired with the unconditioned stimulus (meat powder), is called the conditioned stimulus, and the response it comes to trigger is a learned or **conditioned response (CR)**.

Excerpt, as attached, from *Essentials of Psychology*, by Douglas Bernstein et al, pp. 146–148 © 2002

---

5. *triggers* = allows something to begin; suddenly causes something to happen

ACTIVITY 5   Getting content from a reading

Write answers to these questions about the reading. Be prepared to discuss your answers with your class.

1. What was the strange thing that Pavlov noticed in his experiments on physiology?
2. What were the three phases or steps in the experiment on salivation?
3. In classical conditioning, what causes a change in the response to a neutral stimulus?

POWER GRAMMAR

Cause and Effect Expressions

The lecture you will hear often contains a description of a cause and effect relationship between two events.

> **Example:** As a result of this conditioning, a warm feeling is associated with the product.

In this example, the cause is "this conditioning" and the effect is the "warm feeling is associated with the product." The speaker makes the connection between these two events by using a common cause and effect expression: "As a result of ..."

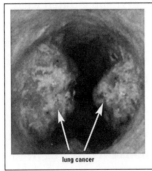

WARNING

CIGARETTES CAUSE LUNG CANCER

85% of lung cancers are caused by smoking. 80% of lung cancer victims die within 3 years.

Health Canada

lung cancer

Many thousands of people worldwide develop lung cancer and heart disease every year as a result of smoking.

There are several other cause and effect expressions and words that you will hear in the lecture:

> when, since
> as a result of, because of
> cause, elicit

(Continued)

Not all of these expressions have the same meaning. For example, "elicit" means "bring something out," which is somewhat different from "cause." However, both words express a basic cause and effect relationship.

In less formal speech, you may hear or use other cause and effect expressions, in addition to the expressions in the list above. For example, **because** and **so** can link two clauses:

I'm hungry because I didn't eat breakfast.

I didn't eat breakfast, so I'm hungry.

I was late because I missed my bus.

I missed my bus, so I was late.

Cause and effect expressions are used to link different kinds of grammatical structures. Some cause and effect expressions link two clauses, some link two noun phrases, and some link a clause and a noun phrase.

Linking Two Clauses: when, since, because

People organized a system for trading **when** other societies had goods they needed.

People organized a system for trading **since** other societies had goods they needed.

People organized a system for trading **because** other societies had goods they needed.

Linking a Noun Phrase and a Clause: as a result of, because of

A new response was noticed **as a result of** the conditioning.

As a result of the conditioning, a new response was noticed.

A new response was noticed **because of** the conditioning.

Linking Two Noun Phrases: cause (v.), elicit

The length of the war **caused** damage to many institutions.

The complaint **elicited** a strong response.

(Continued)

As an academic listener, one of your important jobs is to understand cause and effect connections that speakers make. In a lecture class, you may need to take notes about these connections very quickly, while an instructor is talking. Many students use a short way to express this connection when they are writing notes, by writing *arrows* (like →) between events. For example, this sentence:

> As a result of this conditioning, a warm feeling is associated with the product.

can be summarized like this:

conditioning → warm feeling assoc. w/ product

ACTIVITY 6   **Listening for cause and effect**

Your instructor will give you some examples of sentences that use cause and effect expressions. As you listen, take notes about the cause and the effect. Use arrows and abbreviations, as the example shows. When you are finished, discuss your answers with your class.

Example: The process is repeated, so there is a long-lasting effect.

process is repeated → long-lasting effect

1.

2.

3.

4.

5.

POWER GRAMMAR

Past Participles as Adjectives

Many important words in this lecture are adjectives that come from past participle forms of verbs. In other words, they are past participle forms used as adjectives. Here are some examples:

> This is an example of learned behavior.

> They played the disliked music first.

> A conditioned stimulus may not be present.

These adjective forms are like verbs; they follow the same rules used for pronouncing past participle forms. They are also like adjectives because they appear before a noun. (In the examples above, the nouns are *behavior*, *music*, and *stimulus*.) These forms are also related to passive voice. (You will learn more about passive voice in Chapter 5).

> learn**ed** behavior is: behavior that is learn**ed**

> dislik**ed** music is: music that is dislik**ed**

These adjective forms are very common in academic speech, but you may not hear them often in daily informal speech. They can be difficult to recognize because the endings that mark them as past participles can be difficult to hear.

STRATEGY

Giving Structure to Class Notes

Your most important goal when you listen to a lecture is to understand the main points. One of the challenges in taking notes is giving some structure to your notes. Good notes clearly show the different general topics that are discussed in the lecture, and they show the difference between general points and specific points.

ACTIVITY 7 Listening for different forms of words

Practice recognizing the verb and adjective forms of words in these sentences. Write the words that you hear.

Master Student Tip

▼ Taking notes is not the same as dictation. When you take notes on a lecture, think about the *meaning* of what you hear, and write about what you understand, rather than every word you hear.

1. pair (v.)

    a. They _____ two stimuli.

    b. The _____ become connected.

2. publish (v.)

    a. The _____ had a surprising conclusion.

    b. They _____ their results in a journal.

3. desire (v.)

    a. The _____ was observed.

    b. The researchers _____ the results.

4. learn (v.)

    a. The subjects _____ three trials.

    b. This was an example of a _____.

5. link (v.)

    a. They were _____ stimuli.

    b. The _____ pleasant feelings and

    products.

☐ Getting Information from a Lecture

The lecture you will hear links two fields: psychology and advertising, which is part of the field of marketing. Psychology is the study of human behavior. Marketing is the study of how products are developed and brought into a system of exchange. The lecture discusses a kind of learning called classical conditioning and it shows how this form of learning is important in marketing.

Listening Strategies

One of the challenges in taking notes is giving your notes some structure. Good notes clearly show the different general topics that are discussed in the lecture, and they show the difference between general points and specific points such as examples. When you listen to this chapter's lecture, you should focus on four strategies for taking good notes:

First, **write only important words**, since you do not have time to write sentences.

Second, **use abbreviations and special symbols** for common or repeated words, to save time.

Third, **use symbols (such as "→") to show cause and effect relationships between ideas**.

Fourth, **use a system for showing the difference between general ideas and details**. You should write the most general ideas closer to the left side of the page, and the details and examples closer to the right side of the page.

Here is an example. Imagine that an instructor is giving a talk about advertising and psychology, this chapter's topic. The instructor says this:

> Consumers learn to associate products with positive feelings. For example, they might feel better about one kind of soap than another kind. Or they might associate a certain soft drink with fun or happiness.

If you wanted to take notes on this part of a lecture, you could not write all these words. You would have to choose which words were most important, and you would need to abbreviate some words. You could also arrange the notes to show the difference between general statements and examples. Here are some notes on this example:

Cons assoc prods w/ pos feelings
    Feel better abt one kind of soap
    Assoc soft drink w/ fun/happiness

ACTIVITY 8   **Taking notes from a lecture**

Take notes on the following short excerpts from a psychology lecture. Use the system of writing general points to the left and details to the right. Here is an example:

You hear:

He saw that certain stimuli cause or elicit a response naturally, without any teaching or other experience. He called these unconditioned stimuli. An example of an unconditioned stimulus for a dog would be food.

You might write:

Cert stim elicit resp w/o teaching or exp: uncond stim

ex for dog: food

1.

2.

3.

🎧 **ACTIVITY 9** **Taking notes**

Listen to Parts 1–4 of the lecture. As you listen, use the questions below to guide you. Take notes that answer a question. Use the note-taking skills you practiced in Activity 6 and Activity 8: use arrows (→) to show cause and effect relationships, and write more general ideas to the left. (Space is provided below each question to write your notes. If it is easier, you can write your notes on a separate piece of paper.)

Before you listen, review these "blackboard notes." They show what the instructor writes on the blackboard during the lecture. You can use them as you listen to the lecture to help you follow what the instructor is saying. Your instructor may ask you listen to each part more than one time.

Stimulus or Response:	Definition:	Example:
Unconditioned Stimulus (UCS)	S that naturally elicits response	food
Unconditioned Response (UCR)	R that is elicited by US	salivation
Neutral Stimulus (NS)	S that does not elicit response	bell (before learning)
Conditioned Stimulus (CS)	Previously NS that has been paired with US	bell (after learning)
Conditioned Response (CR)	R that is elicited by CS	salivation (after learning)

Before learning:	In the learning process:	After learning:
UCS → UCR	NS is paired with UCS.	
NS → no response	NS becomes CS.	CS → CR

Part 1. Classical conditioning and people

Why does the instructor say that classical conditioning is important?

_____

_____

What is the topic of the lecture?

_____

_____

Part 2. Classical conditioning and advertising

What do people or animals learn when they learn through classical conditioning?

_____

_____

Why is classical conditioning interesting to people who study advertising?

_____

_____

Part 3. Pavlov's experiment

The first scientist to write about classical conditioning was Pavlov. What was he interested in?

_____

_____

What observations did Pavlov make about stimuli and responses in dogs? What kinds of stimuli and responses did he observe?

_____

_____

_____

_____

_____

_____

Part 4. Classical conditioning and everyday life

What happens when learning takes place through classical conditioning?

_____

_____

ACTIVITY 10 **Learning more about taking useful lecture notes**

Below you will see a good set of notes that use the note-taking strategies you have practiced so far. Study these notes, and compare them to your notes from Activity 9. What are the differences? After comparing the two sets of notes, fill in the chart. Set a goal for improving your note-taking for Parts 5 and 6 of the lecture. After you finish, your instructor may ask you to listen to Parts 1–4 again, to see if you can improve your notes before you go on to Activity 11.

Put a check mark next to any statement that you agree with:

I am satisfied with my notes the way they are	
I can improve my notes by:	
writing fewer words	
writing more words	
using abbreviations and symbols	
showing cause and effect relationships	
showing general points and details	

Why does the instructor say that classical conditioning is important?

> Imp. to learn abt conditioning:
>   aff. things in everyday life

What is the topic of the lecture?

> Topic: Conn. betw psych. and advert.

What do people or animals learn when they learn through classical conditioning?

> People/anims learn emot. resp. to things they don't norm. resp. to

Why is classical conditioning interesting to people who study advertising?

> Adv hopes to create emot. resp to prods.

The first scientist to write about classical conditioning was Pavlov. What was he interested in?

> Basic idea of c.c.:
>   Researcher: Pavlov: physiologist
>   Interested in salivation of dogs, digest. syst.

What observations did Pavlov make about stimuli and responses in dogs? What kinds of stimuli and responses did he observe?

> Observations:
>   stimuli (def. things we can see, hear, feel, etc.) and responses:
>   Unconditioned Stim (US): naturally → resp.
>   e.g., for dog: food
>   Uncond. Resp (UR): resp. to uncond. stim.
>   Example: saliv. in dogs
>   Neutral stim (NS): stim that don't → resp.
>   Ex: for dog, book, picture, song, sound of bell

What happens when learning takes place through classical conditioning?

When learning takes place: neut stim paired w/uncond. stim.
    Example: food (US) paired with sound of bell (NS)
    Bell → cond. stim; resp to bell same way they resp. to food
This cond. applies to human beings also.

This drawing shows the design of a famous experiment of Pavlov about the learning of conditioned responses.

ACTIVITY **11**   **Taking notes**

Listen to Parts 5–6 of the lecture. As you listen, use the questions as an outline. As you answer the questions, use the note-taking skills you practiced in Activity 10.

Part 5. More about classical conditioning and advertising

What does classical conditioning have to do with people?

_____

_____

_____

_____

How is classical conditioning used in advertising?

_____

_____

_____

_____

Part 6. More on Pavlov's experiment

The researchers tested the use of conditioning in an experiment. What was the hypothesis in the experiment?

_____

_____

_____

_____

What was the procedure used in the experiment?

_____

_____

_____

_____

What was the result of the experiment?

_____

_____

_____

_____

☐ After Your First Listening: Clarifying Your Notes

Successful students review their notes after they finish taking them. Often, students compare their notes with their classmates to make sure they understood the lecture's most important points.

Here is an example. Imagine a student is looking at this question about the lecture:

> What observations did Pavlov make about stimuli and responses in dogs? What kinds of stimuli and responses did he observe?

The student was not able to write down the needed information. Perhaps the lecturer was talking too fast, or the student was thinking about something else. In comparing notes with classmates, the student could ask:

> I'm working on the part about the stimuli. What's the US?

Or:

> He said the US naturally causes a response. Then there's an example. What's an example of a US?

ACTIVITY 12 Clarifying your notes

Work with a small group. Discuss the lecture outline for Parts 5–6 with your classmates. Find out if you and your classmates completed the outline in the same way. After your discussion, talk over your answers with your instructor. Add new information to your notes. You will use your notes for assignments later in this chapter.

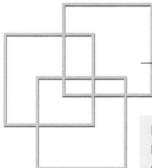

Part 2

EFFECTIVE ACADEMIC SPEAKING

In a lecture class the instructor often does most of the talking. However, students also have very important speaking roles. In this part of the chapter, you will learn about three kinds of academic speaking that students do: explaining what you already know about an academic topic, summarizing part of a lecture, and asking a question for clarification.

☐ Explaining What You Already Know: Practice Speaking with Cause and Effect Expressions

Part of this chapter is about the causes of consumer behavior. In a course on this topic, an instructor might begin by asking students what they already know about the subject. For example, at the beginning of a lecture, an instructor might ask, "So, what are some of the things that cause a consumer to buy one product instead of another?" Students will suggest answers to this question before the lecture begins.

ACTIVITY 13 Using cause and effect

Practice answering a cause and effect question about consumer behavior. Work in a small group. Make a list of things that cause people to buy one product instead of another. After your group has made its list, discuss your answers with your group. Then your instructor will ask students to volunteer to answer the question. You may want to review the list of cause and effect expressions on pages 38–39.

What are some of the things that cause a consumer to buy one product instead of another?

Cause	Effect
the price	people choose to buy a product
they see ads on TV	

Example: People choose to buy a product because of the price.

☐ Speaking About the Lecture

Students in lecture courses often need to give short summaries of a part of a lecture. There are several situations in which this happens. For example, at the beginning of a class, an instructor might ask students to summarize the important points from a previous class. The instructor may do this to check that the previous lecture was clear.

For example, an instructor might start a class by saying:

> Last time we were discussing classical conditioning. Can someone remind us about the different kinds of stimuli and maybe give us some examples?

The most successful students will volunteer to give a short summary that answers the instructor's question.

ACTIVITY 14   **Using lecture notes to prepare a summary**

Use your lecture notes to prepare a short oral summary of part of the lecture. In your summary, include both general points and examples or details. For example, if your notes look like this:

> Unconditioned Stim (US): naturally → resp.
>   e.g. for dog: food

you might say:

> An unconditioned stimulus is a stimulus that naturally causes a response. For example, for a dog, food is an unconditioned stimulus.

Your instructor might ask you to give your summary to a small group or to the whole class.

☐ Asking a Question for Clarification during a Lecture

Every college lecturer has a different style, and every class has its own mood and behavior. However, most lecture classes follow a set of rules for deciding when people speak.

When an instructor is lecturing, students usually allow the instructor to decide who can speak. (This is different from other situations in class, when instructors may ask students to discuss a topic informally, to work in groups, etc.)

In an academic course, you will sometimes need to speak to make sure that you understand the content of what the instructor says. Sometimes you will need to ask a question to make sure you understand. In most lecture situations, students raise their hand to ask a question, and then they wait for the lecturer to give them a sign. The instructor might signal them to wait (sometimes by raising a finger) or to speak (sometimes by pointing at the student, or raising the eyebrows).

When students get to speak during a lecture (sometimes it is called having "the floor"), they might ask the instructor to repeat something, ask for an example, or check their understanding by *paraphrasing* what they heard.

Here is an example of a student question in a lecture:

Instructor

The result, in this case, was that people liked the products better when they were linked to the music they liked. This result supported the idea that people could learn a positive emotional response to a product. In other words, classical conditioning can cause a change in the feelings of consumers.

(To a student who raises her hand): Yes.

Student

So consumers remembered the music when they saw the pen, and they liked the pen because they liked the music?

Instructor

Not exactly. They *connected* the music and the pen, but we really aren't talking about *remembering* here. Memory is different. This is a different kind of learning. Think of it as making a connection or an association between two things, but not really remembering things. OK? Does that make sense?

In this example, the student's question was helpful to the class, including the instructor. The question gave the student a chance to make the topic more clear, it helped the instructor to understand he needed to explain something more clearly, and it probably helped other students, who might have had the same question.

Notice the form of the student's question in this example. It is common in this situation to begin a paraphrase with "so." Also notice that the student's paraphrase has the form of a sentence, except that its intonation is rising, like a yes or no question.

ACTIVITY 15 Making lecture notes accurate

Work in a small group. Review your notes from this chapter's lecture. Find a place in your notes where you are not completely sure about what you heard. Paraphrase what you understood and practice asking a clarification question using your paraphrase.

When you are finished, work as a whole class. Raise your hand and wait for the instructor to give you the floor. Then, ask your paraphrased question.

Example: So a stimulus is something you can feel?

ACTIVITY 16 Relating the lecture to everyday life

You can do this activity if you have time outside of class. Work as part of a group, or as an individual. Find an advertisement in a magazine, newspaper, or on television, that links positive emotional responses to a product. Prepare a presentation on this advertisement. In your presentation, describe the product, the medium in which the product was advertised, the stimuli in the ad, and the emotional responses that are connected to the stimuli. Describe whether you think the ad is effective, and why or why not.

Part 3

ASSESSING YOUR ACADEMIC LISTENING
AND SPEAKING SKILLS

Marilyn Monroe in the movie
Gentlemen Prefer Blondes,
in which she sings the song,
"Diamonds Are a Girl's Best
Friend"

Whoopi Goldberg dressed
as Queen Elizabeth I of
England, wearing over
$40 million worth of
diamonds for the Academy
Awards show in 1999

☐ A Lecture and Preparing for a Lecture Test

 ACTIVITY 17 Taking notes on a lecture

Listen to this short lecture. Take notes as you listen. If your instructor is reading or performing the lecture, practice asking questions during the lecture that will help your understanding. Make sure you wait for a sign from the instructor before you speak.

These are the names of people and companies that are used as examples in the lecture:

To Catch a Thief	Cartier
Grace Kelly	Tiffany
Gentlemen Prefer Blondes	Henry Winston
Marilyn Monroe	Whoopi Goldberg
"Diamonds Are a Girl's Best Friend"	DeBeers

ACTIVITY 18 Using notes to prepare for a test

After you listen to the short lecture, study your notes. Work in a small group and prepare for a test on the lecture. In your group, make a list of questions you might expect to see on the test. Discuss answers to these questions in your group. Your instructor will ask you to report your questions and answers to the whole class.

After you are done, your teacher will give you a test on the lecture you heard.

☐ Preparing a Short Oral Summary

ACTIVITY 19 Preparing a summary of a lecture

Imagine your instructor asked for a short oral summary of this talk as a review. Work on your own. Listen to the short talk about marketing diamonds. As you are listening, identify one or more examples of:

a neutral stimulus:

_____

_____

an unconditioned stimulus

_____

_____

an unconditioned response

_____

_____

the pairing of neutral and unconditioned stimuli

_____

_____

a conditioned stimulus

_____

_____

a conditioned response

_____

_____

Prepare to summarize the talk, and to explain each stimulus and response in the list above. Your instructor might ask you to give your oral summary in a small group or to the whole class.

☐ Assessing Your Speaking

ACTIVITY 20 **Getting feedback on your speaking skills**

Your instructor will use this checklist to let you know about your use of academic English in your speaking assignment.

Summary of the lecture	OK	Needs work	Example(s)
Content:			
▪ accurately summarized the lecture			
▪ gave appropriate examples			
Organization:			
▪ distinguished general ideas and details			
Vocabulary:			
▪ used academic vocabulary appropriately			
Speaking Grammar:			
▪ used cause and effect expressions correctly			
▪ used participles correctly			

☐ Self-Assessment

ACTIVITY 21   **Evaluating your progress**

Review this list of chapter objectives. Think about your work and progress in each of these areas. Make a check mark after objectives that need your special attention in future work on academic speaking and listening.

- Learn the stress pattern and meaning of new academic vocabulary _____

- Recognize and take notes on cause and effect expressions _____

- Recognize and understand past participles used as adjectives _____

- Take notes on a lecture's main points and details _____

- Compare and clarify lecture notes with classmates _____

- Speak with cause and effect expressions _____

- Summarize a lecture's important points _____

- Ask questions for clarification during a lecture _____

- Prepare for a lecture test _____

- Prepare a short oral summary _____

Look back at this list after you finish the work in the next chapter.

W E B   P O W E R

You will find additional exercises related to the content in this chapter at **http://esl.college.hmco.com/students.**

Survival of the Fittest on the World Wide Web

ACADEMIC FOCUS: BUSINESS ▶ E-COMMERCE

Academic Listening and Speaking Objectives

In this chapter, you will learn some of the language skills that are important in a business course on electronic commerce, or e-commerce. In part of the chapter, you will learn about listening to a formal lecture. In another part, you will learn about working with classmates to give an oral report. The lecture's topic is the use of the Internet to market products.

Objectives are to:

- Recognize syllable stress in academic word families
- Recognize examples in a lecture
- Understand information about class assignments
- Take notes on a lecture's important points and details
- Summarize a lecture's main points
- Summarize information from a chart
- Summarize a case study

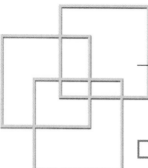

Part 1

EFFECTIVE ACADEMIC LISTENING

☐ **Getting Ready for Academic Listening**

ACTIVITY 1 Discussing a lecture's content

This chapter is about using the Internet to market products. Work in a small group to discuss these questions.

1. Discuss your own experience with the World Wide Web. Have you used a computer to connect to the Web? If yes, what kind of websites have you visited? Do you remember advertisements that you have seen on the Web? What products have you seen?

2. Which of these products would you consider buying from a World Wide Web site? Discuss why or why not.

   car   plane ticket
   book   medical advice
   shoes   computer hardware

3. Have you bought anything through the World Wide Web? What was it? How much did you spend? Was it better for you to use the Web for your purchase? If so, why?

This advertisement for Garden.com, an online garden supply company, appeared in 1998 in Horticulture, a magazine for gardeners. Garden.com is an example of an online business that failed.

ACTIVITY 2 Analyzing the stress pattern of vocabulary

The words that follow are important in the lecture you will hear. Some of them may be new to you. Most of them are from the Academic Word List. Find the words in your dictionary, and be prepared to pronounce them correctly. Use the system for noting the number of syllables and the stressed syllables that you learned in Chapter 1, page 4. (Record the numbers within the brackets that look like this: [___ - ___]. Your instructor may ask you to pronounce these words before you hear the lecture.

Example:

commerce [_2_ - _1_]

(This means that *commerce* has two syllables and that the first syllable is stressed. This information should help you pronounce *commerce* correctly.)

1. firm (n.) [___ - ___]
2. investor [___ - ___]
3. competition [___ - ___]
4. principle [___ - ___]
5. element [___ - ___]

6. project (n.) [___ - ___]
7. promote [___ - ___]
8. distribute [___ - ___]
9. issue (v.) [___ - ___]
10. bond [___ - ___]

ACTIVITY 3 Analyzing syllable-stress

Listen to your instructor pronounce these words. Use the notation system to record the number of syllables and the stressed syllable. When you finish, review your answers with your instructor.

1. traditional [___ - ___]
2. tangible [___ - ___]
3. financial [___ - ___]
4. focus [___ - ___]
5. available [___ - ___]

6. ignore [___ - ___]
7. process [___ - ___]
8. invest [___ - ___]
9. assignment [___ - ___]
10. rely [___ - ___]

ACTIVITY 4 **Working with academic vocabulary**

Learn the meanings of the academic words that are used in this chapter. First, match each of the following words with the phrase that is closest to the word's meaning. Then review your answers with your class. For words you do not know, get help from your dictionary or your instructor. Use the answers for this activity to study the meanings.

1. assignment ____
2. available ____
3. bond ____
4. competition ____
5. distribute ____
6. element ____
7. financial ____
8. firm (n.) ____
9. focus (v.) ____
10. ignore ____

11. invest ____
12. investor ____
13. issue (v.) ____
14. principle ____
15. process ____
16. project (n.) ____
17. promote ____
18. rely ____
19. tangible ____
20. traditional ____

a. related to money
b. let people know something good about something
c. a person who puts money into a business
d. a job given to someone
e. following the old, usual way
f. basic rule
g. piece of work that is done over time
h. depend; be sure that something will happen
i. bring to various places
j. a kind of loan; an investment in which someone loans money

k. the steps in doing something
l. a business
m. physical; can be touched
n. pay the most attention to
o. trying to do the same thing as someone else, but better
p. not to pay attention
q. part
r. possible to get
s. put money into a business, with the hope that more money will be returned
t. give out or send out

ACTIVITY 5   **Analyzing word forms**

The verbs in the list in Activity 4 belong to a group or "family" of words. This family includes words that have the same basic meaning, but different forms according to whether they act as nouns, verbs, adjectives, or adverbs in a sentence. For example, the verb *consume* is in the vocabulary list. When you learn *consume*, you should also learn other forms in the same family, such as *consumer* (a person who consumes) and *consumption* (the act of consuming).

Notice the stress patterns in these noun forms also. *Consumer* and *consumption* both have three syllables, and both have the main, or primary, stress on the second syllable.

The following list of verbs and nouns appear in this chapter's lecture. In every case, the verbs have a [2-2] stress pattern and the nouns have a [3-2] stress pattern. As you study new vocabulary in this book, you will be asked to notice the stress pattern of other members of the word's family.

Verbs [2-2]	Nouns [3-2]
consume	consumer, consumption
promote	promoter, promotion
create	creator, creation
invest	investor, investment

Listen to your teacher read each of these sentences. Write the missing words in the blank. One of the words is from the vocabulary list on page 66. After you finish, read aloud what you have written.

1. Increases in income lead to an increase _____ of goods.

2. _____ about products on a company's website.

3. Companies _____ services easily on the Web.

4. _____ expensive goods on the Web is often not successful.

5. Using the Web for retail sales requires _____ building a physical store.

6. Many people _____ online companies in the 1990s lost money.

7. E-commerce companies can _____ images through their websites.

8. The _____ is part of a marketing system.

CheapTickets.com uses this website to allow consumers to buy airline and other tickets without visiting a travel office.

**Master
Student Tip**

▼ Reading a
textbook chapter
before a lecture
will help you
understand new
words and
information.

ACTIVITY 6 Using your text to prepare for a lecture

*The following passage is from a textbook that is used in a business course.
Read the passage, and make note of its important ideas. As you read, find
out the meaning of words that interest you.*

THE DYNAMIC NATURE OF ELECTRONIC MARKETING

1 In this chapter, we focus on how the Internet, especially the
World Wide Web, relates to all aspects of marketing, including
strategic planning. Thus, we use the term electronic marketing (or
e-marketing) to refer to the strategic process of creating,
distributing, promoting, and pricing products for targeted
customers in the virtual environment of the Internet.

2   One of the most important benefits of e-marketing is the ability
of marketers and customers to share information. Through
company websites, consumers can learn about a firm's products,
including features, specifications, and even prices. Many websites
also provide feedback mechanisms through which customers can
ask questions, voice complaints, indicate preferences, and
otherwise communicate about their needs and desires. The Internet
has changed the way marketers communicate and develop
relationships not only with their customers but also with their
employees and suppliers. Many companies use e-mail, groupware
(software that allows people in different locations to access and
work on the same file or document over the Internet), and
videoconferencing to coordinate activities and communicate with
employees. Because such technology facilitates and lowers the cost
of communications, the Internet can contribute significantly to any
industry or activity that depends on the flow of information, such
as entertainment, health care, government services, education,
travel services, and software.

3   Telecommunications technology offers additional benefits to
marketers, including rapid response expanded customer service
capability (e.g., 24 hours a day, 7 days a week, or "24 × 7"),
decreased operating costs, and reduced geographic barriers. Data
networks have decreased cycle and decision times and permitted

companies to treat customers more efficiently. In today's fast-paced world, the ability to shop for books, clothes, and other merchandise at midnight, when traditional stores are usually closed, is a benefit for both buyers and sellers. The Internet allows even small firms to reduce the impact of geography on their operations. For example, Coastal Tool & Supply, a small power tool and supply store in Connecticut, has generated sales from around the world through its website.

4   Despite these benefits, many companies that chose to make the Internet the core of their marketing strategies— often called "dot-coms"— failed to earn profits or acquire sufficient resources to remain in business. Even Amazon.com, the world's leading online retailer, continues to struggle to earn a profit. The table on page 70 lists a sampling of failed Internet-based companies. In some cases, their brand names, once backed by millions of promotional dollars, have been acquired by competitors that appreciate the strong brand equity these names represent. KB Toys, for example, purchased the name and inventory of the defunct Web retailer eToys.

5   Many dot-coms failed because they thought the only thing that mattered was brand awareness. In reality, however, Internet markets are more similar to traditional markets than they are different. Thus, successful e-marketing strategies, like traditional marketing ones, depend on creating, distributing, promoting, and pricing products that customers need or want, not merely developing a brand name or reducing the costs associated with online transactions. In fact, traditional retailers continue to do quite well in some areas that many people thought the Internet would dominate just a few years ago. For example, although many marketers believed there would be a shift to buying cars online, experts predict that just 3 percent of all new cars will be sold through the Internet in 2003. Research suggests that online shoppers are very concerned about price, and a firm's profits can vanish quickly as competition drives prices down. Few consumers are willing to spend $30,000 online to purchase a new automobile. However, consumers are increasingly making car-buying decisions on the basis of information found online.

6   Indeed, e-marketing has not changed all industries, although it has had more of an impact in some industries in which the costs of business and customer transactions are very high. For example, trading stock has become significantly easier and less expensive for customers who can go online and execute their own orders. Firms such as E*Trade and Charles Schwab have been innovators in this area, and traditional brokerage firms such as Merrill Lynch have had to introduce online trading for their customers to remain competitive. In many other industries, however, the impact of e-marketing may be incremental.

William Pride and O.C. Ferrell, *Marketing: Concepts and Strategies*, Twelfth Edition. Copyright © 2003 by Houghton Mifflin Company. Reprinted with permission.

A dot-com graveyard	
Company	**Primary product**
eToys	toys
FoodUSA.com	meat and poultry exchange
More.com	health products
Garden.com	gardening products
Hardware.com	home improvement
Pets.com	pet products
Furniture.com	furniture
Beautyscene.com	fashion and cosmetics
Auctions.com	online auction

Source: "Welcome to the Dot-Com Graveyard," Upside Today, www.upside.com/graveyard, Aug. 8, 2001. *In Marketing* by Pride and Farrell, Houghton Mifflin 2003.

ACTIVITY 7 Getting content from a reading

Write answers to these questions about the textbook passage. Be prepared to give your answer orally to the whole class.

1. What is the definition of *marketing* in this passage?
2. In paragraph 2, what are three groups that marketers can communicate with using the Internet?
3. What kinds of industries can lower their costs by using technology for communication?
4. In paragraph 3, what are examples of ways that telecommunications can make things more convenient for customers?
5. Why do car retailers not sell many cars through the Internet? What advantage can the Internet give to car sellers?
6. How has Internet stock trading affected traditional trading companies?

☐ Getting Information from a Lecture: Taking Notes

The lecture you will hear in this chapter is about using the World Wide Web to market products. As in Chapter 1, your listening should include:

- making notes while the instructor is talking; your notes will help you remember what the instructor said
- making notes about course assignments

As you learned in Chapters 1 and 2, a few principles or rules will help you make better notes:

- Only write content words (verbs, nouns, adjectives, and adverbs) and sometimes prepositions (such as *to, in, at*) in your notes.
- Write abbreviations for long words.
- Make your own set of easy symbols for words that are used often.
- Use a system to show the difference between general ideas and details or examples.

ACTIVITY 8   **Taking lecture notes**

Your instructor will give you some examples of sentences that you will hear in a lecture in this chapter. As you listen, make notes. Write only the important words, and use abbreviations for common words. When you finish, discuss your answers with your class. Your classmates might have some good ideas about abbreviations that you can use.

Example:

We have to follow the same principles that we follow in any other kind of business.

Foll. same pric. as in other bus.

Notes:

1.

2.

3.

4.

5.

POWER GRAMMAR

Examples

This lecture's speaker describes some of the general features in electronic commerce. To make these features more clear, the speaker also gives examples of companies that show these features. Here is part of the lecture you will hear:

> E-commerce can succeed, particularly in some industries. For example, the United States government is the world's biggest online retailer, and its online sales of bonds and so on are very successful. Two examples of online companies that have made money are Amazon.com, the bookseller, and eBay, the online auction company.

In this part of the lecture, a student has to understand two things: the general point, and the examples that help explain the general point. In this example, the speaker's general point is:

> E-commerce can succeed, particularly in some industries.

The examples are:

> For example, the United States government is the world's biggest online retailer, and its online sales of bonds are very successful.

and:

> Two examples of online companies that have made money are Amazon.com, the bookseller, and eBay, the online auction company.

Very often, speakers use a phrase like *for example* to introduce an example that is given in a sentence.

> For example, *the United States government is the world's biggest online retailer.*

↑

Sentence

(Continued)

In other cases, a speaker might use *an example . . . is* to introduce a noun phrase.

An example of an online company that has made money is *Amazon.com, the bookseller.*

Noun phrase

You should have a set of symbols to record examples in your lecture notes. Many people use *e.g.,* a Latin abbreviation meaning *for example.* Often, people write notes about details or examples farther to the right side of the page. This is to show that they are more specific than the general point, which is written on the left side. Notes on the passage above might look like this:

E-comm can succeed:

e.g. U.S. gov.: largest online retailer

Amazon.com: bookseller

ACTIVITY 9   Taking notes on examples

You will hear short passages that include examples. Listen to the passages, and make notes about what you hear. Use abbreviations, and make notes about the examples. When you are finished, discuss your answers with your class. Here is an example:

> Some online companies have made money. For example, eBay and Amazon are profitable.

> Some online co. made $:
>
>   e.g., eBay, Amazon

Notes:

1.

2.

3.

4.

5.

STRATEGY

Understanding Instructions for Class Assignments

Instructors often give written instructions for class assignments, and most instructors also give information about assignments orally in class. Sometimes this information includes important details about the assignment. In making notes from oral instructions, make sure you have detailed information about the task to be done, the resources to be used, the deadline or due date, and the standards to be used for the assignment, such as the length or the form.

☐ Understanding Instructions for Class Assignments

Some instructions for assignments in academic courses are written for you. Your assignments may be written in a syllabus or course description that you receive at the beginning of a course. Your instructors also might give you written assignments during the semester. In addition, instructors also give information about assignments orally in class. Sometimes this information includes important details about the assignment. Here is an example of part of a discussion about an assignment that you will hear as part of this chapter's lecture.

Instructor

> I'd like to talk to you about the this chapter's project. I'm asking you to do a case study of an e-business. I wrote about this assignment in the syllabus, but I'd like to explain. You have some written descriptions of businesses that I gave you last week. First you're going to read the description of the company you are studying. You can get more information by searching the Web if you like, but there should be enough information here. Then you're going to prepare a talk about one of the businesses.

In this part of the talk the instructor gives some important information about the assignment. He tells what resources students are supposed to use, and what task the students are supposed to do.

After some questions from students, the instructor also gives other information, including the deadline or due date for the work, and the standards the instructor will use to evaluate the work, including the amount and content of the work. For example:

Student

How long does it have to be?

Instructor

Well I'm mostly concerned about the content and not the length. Make sure you discuss distributing, promoting, and pricing. I think that will take about ten minutes, don't you? If you talk for less than ten minutes, something is wrong, OK? On the other hand, please don't go on for an hour. I'd say ten to fifteen minutes is good. Anything else?

Student

When is it due?

Instructor

We're going to start these in class next week, starting on Tuesday. I hope we can get to five a day, and I hope we can finish in four class meetings.

In this example, the students are very important in the exchange of information, and this is very common. When college students feel they do not have enough information about the tasks, resources, deadline, and standards for an assignment, they will take action to get the information.

In this example, we could summarize the information about the assignment like this:

Business case study assignment			
Task	**Resource**	**Deadline**	**Standards**
prepare a talk about a business	written descriptions; World Wide Web	next Tuesday, or next three class meetings after that	discuss distributing, promoting, pricing; talk for 10–15 minutes

ACTIVITY 10   Listening for class assignments

You will hear an example of instructions for a class assignment. As you listen, take notes about the task, resources, deadline, and standards for the assignment. After you finish, discuss your notes with your class.

Task	Resource	Deadline	Standards

ACTIVITY 11   Listening to a lecture and taking notes

**Master
Student Tip**

When you take notes on a lecture, don't write complete sentences; use "shortcuts" to save time.

Now you will listen to a lecture and take notes that will help you remember what you heard.

The outline below has a list of important questions about the lecture you will hear. Review these questions with your class before you listen. Make sure you understand the questions, even if you do not know the answers. Then, while you are listening, try to write answers to the questions. Use the note-taking skills you practiced in Activity 8 and Activity 9. Some of the notes are started for you.

The outline is divided into parts or sections. Your instructor will decide how many parts of the lecture to work with before you stop to review your notes.

When you finish this activity, you will have a good set of notes about the lecture.

Part 1. Goal of the class meeting

What are the goals for this class?

_____

_____

Part 2. Marketing principles

What is the definition of marketing?

_____

_____

_____

Part 3. E-Marketing failures

Why did so many e-marketing companies fail?

_____

_____

_____

Why did Garden.com fail?

_____

_____

Part 4. Successful e-commerce companies

What are examples of e-commerce firms that succeeded?

_____

_____

What types of products are most likely to sell online?

_____

_____

What types of products are less likely to sell online? What is an exception to this?

_____

_____

_____

_____

Part 5. Distributing products online

Electronic communication can provide an advantage in distributing products. What is an example of this advantage? What is an example of a business that has used this advantage?

_____

_____

_____

Part 6. Promoting products online

People who visit a website are more willing to spend time learning about a new product. What is an example of an industry that uses this advantage?

_____

_____

_____

Part 7. Pricing products online

Why did online companies initially think they could cut costs by using the Internet? What was the problem with this strategy?

_____

_____

_____

_____

What is an example of an industry that was not able to lower prices by using the Internet?

_____

_____

ACTIVITY 12 Reviewing lecture notes

Work with a partner and review the notes you made on the outline in Activity 11. Discuss what you wrote. You may want to make changes in your notes after you discuss them with your partner. Then review the textbook reading for this chapter. You may wish to add information from the text to help you answer the questions in the outline. You will use these notes later.

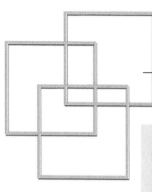

Part 2

EFFECTIVE ACADEMIC SPEAKING

In speaking about academic topics, both students and teachers give examples to make their points more clear. In this section, you will practice summarizing important general points and giving examples to explain ideas from the material you have heard and read.

ACTIVITY 13 Getting information from lecture notes

Work in a small group. Review your notes from Activity 11. Find places in the notes where an example explains a general point. (Many times, the example will begin with e.g.) Then use the notes to describe the general point and the example to other group members. Your instructor will ask you to share an example from your group with the whole class. Here is an example (from Part 4):

> e-comm. successes:
>
> > e.g., U.S. gov.: bonds
> >
> > Amazon.com: books
> >
> > eBay: auctions

Some e-commerce businesses succeeded. For example, the U.S. government sells bonds through the Internet. Another example is Amazon.com. It sells books. Another example is eBay, the auction company.

ACTIVITY 14 Analyzing information in a table

This table shows information about a number of e-marketing companies. The table lists a type of company, a product the company offers, and a place to record information about how the company can use the Internet to market the product successfully. Work with a partner. Discuss the information in the chart. Think of how each company can use the Internet to market a product more successfully. Write notes about your examples in the spaces in the chart. When you finish, report your discussion to the class.

Example:

An automobile company can use the Internet to promote cars. For example, a carmaker might advertise a website in a magazine about cars. When people visit the site, they might find more information that might make them more interested in buying a new car.

Type of company	Product	Can use the Internet to:		
		distribute	**promote**	**price**
automobile company	car			
music company	music CD			
clothing company	clothing			
car repair service	car maintenance			
florist	flower arrangements			
airline	plane tickets			
magazine publisher	news magazines			

ACTIVITY 15   Analyzing and reporting on a case study

A case study is an example of one real-life situation in which ideas from part of a course can be discussed. In a business course case study, students are asked to read about a particular business and report its strengths and weaknesses. In their discussion, students are expected to use ideas that have been studied in the course.

In this activity, you will discuss a simple e-business case study. You will work by yourself. First, read the information in the four cases, and choose one of the cases. Then, prepare a short talk about how you think the business in that case will perform. Discuss the case in terms of how well the business can distribute, promote, and price its product. You can organize your notes like this:

Company	Product	Distribute?	Promote?	Price?

In your notes, you can record information that relates to marketing elements. Do you think the business will be able to use the Internet to distribute the product? How? Will the business be able to promote the product? And so on.

Case Study 1

Ebooks is an Internet bookseller. The company maintains a website that allows customers to search for books by title, subject, and author. The site also allows customers to read short passages from books that interest them. The website has an online order form, which allows customers to order books at any time. The books are shipped when the order is received. The company does not have any stores besides the website, so it has only bought one building that is used to handle its business all over the United States.

Case Study 2

National Motors is a car manufacturer. It maintains a website that shows new models of cars. The website is advertised in magazines that likely car buyers read, such as *Street and Road*, *Car News*, etc. Customers can use the website to see a picture of a car in any color or style. The site also allows the customer to compare information about the various car models made by National Motors. The company does not use the site to take orders for cars. Customers must visit a retail store to test-drive the cars, to discuss car payments, etc.

Case Study 3

Cosmos is an Internet travel agency. The company maintains a website that allows customers to buy airline tickets and package tours, and reserve hotel rooms and car rentals. The site allows customers to search for the best prices from many different companies. There is a $5 service charge for each ticket that Cosmos sells. Customers pay by credit card. Then they print out their tickets and receipts. The company does not have any stores.

Case Study 4

Clear-Skin is a health-related company. It maintains a website that displays information about its skin- and hair-care products. The website advertises in magazines that health-care customers read, such as *Sixteen* and *Health Digest*. On the website, customers can read about products that help control skin and hair problems. The site also offers customers statements written by doctors and satisfied customers. The Clear-Skin site uses an online order form, and accepts payment by credit card. The company does not have retail stores.

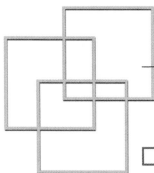

Part 3

☐ Listening to a Short Lecture

ACTIVITY 16 Listening to a lecture and taking notes

Listen to the short lecture that follows. While listening, take notes on the important points.

Look at the "blackboard notes" while you listen. These notes show what an instructor writes on the blackboard to help students during class. The blackboard notes will help you follow the lecture's content, and will help with recognizing vocabulary. You can use the blackboard notes as part of your own notes. When you finish listening, your instructor will test you on what you heard. Your instructor may ask to see both your notes and your answers to the questions.

> E-commerce: produce
> distribute
> promote
> price
>
> Internet
> E-comm. companies:
> Toys.com
> eBay
> U.S. Postal Service
> record industry

ACTIVITY 17 Using lecture notes to prepare for tests

Listen to the following description of an assignment for a business class. As you listen, take notes that will help you remember the important parts of the instructions. When you finish, answer the questions that follow. Your instructor may ask you to write your answers on a piece of paper and hand them in.

1. What work are students supposed to do?

   _____

   _____

2. What information should students include in the assignment?

   _____

   _____

3. When is the assignment due?

   _____

   _____

4. How long is the assignment supposed to be?

   _____

   _____

ACTIVITY 18 Reviewing notes to prepare an oral summary

Review your notes from Activity 16, and prepare to summarize the talk. Your instructor might ask you to give your oral summary in a small group or to the whole class.

☐ **Assessing Your Speaking**

ACTIVITY 19 **Getting feedback on your speaking skills**

Your instructor may use this checklist to discuss your use of academic English in your speaking assignments.

Case study	OK	Needs work	Example(s)
Content:			
▪ discussed distributing, promoting, pricing			
▪ gave appropriate examples			
Organization:			
▪ distinguished general points and examples			
Vocabulary:			
▪ used stress appropriately in academic vocabulary			
Speaking grammar:			
▪ used expressions for examples correctly			

☐ **Self-Assessment**

ACTIVITY 20 **Evaluating your progress**

Review this list of chapter objectives. Think about your work and progress in each of these areas. Make a check mark after objectives that need your special attention in future work on academic speaking and listening.

- ▪ Recognize syllable stress in academic word families _____

- ▪ Recognize examples in a lecture _____

- ▪ Understand information about class assignments _____

- ▪ Take notes on a lecture's important points and details _____

- ▪ Summarize a lecture's main points _____

- ▪ Summarize information from a chart _____

- ▪ Summarize a case study _____

Look back at this list after you finish the work in the next chapter.

WEB POWER

You will find additional exercises related to the content in this chapter at http://esl.college.hmco.com/students.

Chapter

4

Reaching Out
Across Cultures

ACADEMIC FOCUS: SOCIOLOGY

Academic Listening and Speaking Objectives

In this chapter, you will learn some of the language skills that are important in an introductory sociology course. In part of the chapter, you will learn about listening to a formal lecture. In another part, you will learn about working with classmates to give an oral report. The lecture's topic is the study of cultural values.

Objectives are to:

- Recognize syllable stress in academic word families
- Recognize and produce word forms in a word family
- Take notes on important points in a lecture
- Summarize quantitative information from a chart
- Summarize a lecture's main points
- Use academic social rules for politeness

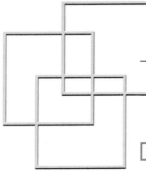

Part 1

☐ Getting Ready for Academic Listening

ACTIVITY 1 Discussing the content of a lecture

This chapter is about the cultural values that affect people's behavior. Values are ideas about what is considered good or proper in a society.

These are examples of values that are discussed in the chapter:

personal success   freedom
hard work   patriotism
humanitarianism[1]   self-fulfillment
progress[2]   preventing others from losing face[3]
loyalty to friends   egalitarianism[4]
respect for elders   practicality
directness in communication   efficiency
respect for authority

Work in a group. Discuss the importance of these values to each person in the group. Your instructor can help you with meanings of words or phrases that are not clear. Each person should rate the importance of each value, using a scale of 1 to 5. A "1" means that this value is most important to the person, and a "5" means this value is least important. Use the roles for working in groups described in Chapter 1. You can use the chart on the next page to record the answers given by group members.

1. *humanitarianism* = a belief in giving help to other people, especially when they are in trouble
2. *progress* = here, the value that society should always improve
3. *preventing others from losing face* = protecting people's positive image of themselves
4. *egalitarianism* = the belief that all people are equal

Value	Rating (1–5)				
	Person 1	Person 2	Person 3	Person 4	Person 5
personal success					
hard work					
humanitarianism					
progress					
loyalty to friends					
respect for elders					
directness in communication					
respect for authority					
freedom					
patriotism					
self-fulfillment					
preventing others from losing face					
egalitarianism					
practicality					
efficiency					

Answer the following questions.

1. Which values seemed most important to group members? In other words, which values got the greatest number of "1" ratings?
2. Which values seemed least important to group members? Which values got the greatest number of "5" ratings?
3. Do you notice that your answers are different from the answers of other group members? How are your answers different?

ACTIVITY 2 Analyzing syllable-stress

The fifteen words that follow are important in the lecture you will hear. Some of them may be new to you. Most of them are from the Academic Word List. Find the words in your dictionary, and be prepared to pronounce them correctly. Use the system learned in Chapter 1 to note the number of syllables and the stressed syllables. (Record the numbers within the brackets that look like this: [___ - ___]. Your instructor may ask you to pronounce these words before you hear the lecture.

Example:

loyalty   [_3_ - _1_]

(This means that *loyalty* has three syllables and the stress is on the first syllable. This information should help you pronounce *loyalty* correctly.)

1. acquire [___ - ___]
2. author [___ - ___]
3. challenging [___ - ___]
4. communication [___ - ___]
5. complex [___ - ___]
6. concept [___ - ___]
7. consists [___ - ___]
8. culture [___ - ___]
9. definitions [___ - ___]
10. derived [___ - ___]
11. distinct [___ - ___]
12. dominate [___ - ___]
13. pattern [___ - ___]
14. practical [___ - ___]
15. tend [___ - ___]

ACTIVITY 3 Analyzing word pronunciation

Listen to your instructor pronounce these words. Use the notation system to record the number of syllables and the stressed syllable. When you finish, review your answers with your instructor.

1. ethnic [___ - ___]

2. global [___ - ___]

3. hierarchy [___ - ___]

4. individualism [___ - ___]

5. infer [___ - ___]

6. interaction [___ - ___]

7. norm [___ - ___]

8. philosophy [___ - ___]

9. physical [___ - ___]

10. positive [___ - ___]

11. sociology [___ - ___]

12. specific [___ - ___]

13. status [___ - ___]

14. survive [___ - ___]

15. vary [___ - ___]

ACTIVITY 4   **Working with academic vocabulary**

Learn the meanings of the academic words used in this chapter. First, match each of the following words with the phrase on the next page that is closest to the word's meaning. Then review your answers with your class. For words you do not know, get help from your dictionary or your instructor. Use the answers for this activity to study the meanings.

1. acquire _____

2. challenging _____

3. communication _____

4. complex _____

5. concept _____

6. consists _____

7. culture _____

8. definitions _____

9. derive _____

10. distinct _____

11. dominate _____

12. ethnic _____

13. global _____

14. hierarchy _____

15. individualism _____

16. infer _____

17. interaction _____

18. norm _____

19. philosophy _____

20. physical _____

21. sociology _____

22. specific _____

23. status _____

24. survive _____

25. tend _____

26. vary _____

a. having many parts
b. covering the world, or covering everything
c. get
d. way of life in a particular society
e. a belief that each person has the right to decide how to live
f. be the biggest or most important
g. connection or communication between people
h. change, including increase and decrease
i. related to things that can be touched, seen, etc.
j. idea
k. a system with some people or things with a place at the top, bottom, etc.

l. difficult
m. not general
n. place or role in a system
o. meanings
p. to live, even in a difficult situation
q. related to a particular group of people
r. a system of ideas or knowledge
s. change in a certain direction
t. different
u. trading information
v. get understanding indirectly by putting together information
w. is made of
x. a rule about what is correct or expected
y. come from
z. the science that studies people in groups

☐ Word Forms

In Chapter 1, you learned about the history of money. In the lecture, you heard about economic needs, problems, and solutions in sentences like this:

They needed to know the metal was **pure**.
There was no **standard** weight.
The commodities had to be **secure**.
It was **easy** to move pure metal long distances.

In each of these sentences, one of the important words in describing the need, problem, or solution is an adjective:

pure   standard   secure   easy

These adjectives occur either after *be* or other non-action verbs such as *seem*, or before a noun.

In some parts of the lecture, the same ideas were expressed by making the need, problem, or solution a noun:

Money solved the problem of **purity**.
Money solved the problem by providing **standardization**.
Trading metal solved the problem of **security**.
The **ease** of hiding money was an advantage.

These nouns occur as the subject of sentences, as direct objects, and after prepositions. In order to know these words well, you need to know the other members of the same "family" of words, that is, other related words that may have different forms because they are used as different parts of speech.

For example, the cultural values discussed in this chapter are expressed as nouns. (The stress pattern is also shown to help you with pronunciation):

loyalty [3-1]   egalitarianism [8-4]   respect [2-2]
efficiency [4-2]   honesty [3-1]   practicality [5-3]

Each of these words also has an adjective form:

loyal [2-1]   egalitarian [6-4]   respectful [3-2]
efficient [3-2]   honest [2-1]   practical [3-1]

After you learn a new word, you should be prepared to understand several members of the same word family.

ACTIVITY 5 **Listening for word forms**

Listen to your instructor read each of these sentences. Write the missing words in the blank. One of the words is a word from the vocabulary list on page 96. Use the correct adjective or noun form of the word. After you finish, read aloud what you wrote.

1. Leaders in that culture often base decisions on _____.

2. Workers there believe that it is more important to be

   _____ of authority.

3. It's an example of an _____ society.

4. _____ is a more important value than respect

   for tradition.

5. They place a high value on _____ in communication.

6. Sometimes there is a conflict between respect for authority and

   _____.

7. Employers and employees are expected to be _____

   to each other.

8. Cultures that value _____ for authority may not

   value _____.

Master Student Tip

▼ When you answer a question from a reading, try to paraphrase what you read, rather than quoting.

ACTIVITY 6   **Using your text to prepare for a lecture**

The following passage is from a textbook used in a sociology course. Read the passage. You may want to note important ideas in the passage, or find out the meaning of words that interest you.

KEY ELEMENTS OF CULTURE

Although cultural traits and complexes vary from society to society, all cultures consist of the same key elements: values, norms, symbols, and knowledge and beliefs.

Values

We each have our own personal values that shape our behavior. One person may value physical fitness and concentrate on running or working out in the gym. Another may value contributing to the community and may spend time helping out in the senior center. Whatever the differences in their personal values, if these two are part of the same culture, they share a general set of objectives as members of their society.

Cultural values are a collection of what is considered good, desirable, and proper in a culture. They reflect what people in a culture prefer as well as what they find morally right. Values are broad, abstract concepts that form the foundation for a whole way of life. The types of values held by a society help determine almost everything else about the culture.

Norms

Two people greet each other as they pass on the sidewalk. One says, "Good morning, how are you?"

"Good morning. How do you like this beautiful weather?"

"I love it. We'd better enjoy it while we can!"

What are they doing? What does their exchange mean? They are acknowledging their acquaintance according to the norms of U.S. society.

Norms are the guidelines people follow in their relations with one another. They are shared standards of desirable behavior. Every society has many norms. These range from small things (Don't eat peanut butter from a knife.) to major things (Do not kill another human being.).

American Values

Each country has its own blend of cultural values that makes it different in some ways from all others. Some values have shaped the United States for many generations, whereas others are emerging and changing as our culture changes.

Traditional American Values

Traditional American values have influenced many generations of Americans. These include success, work, moral concern and humanitarianism, efficiency, progress, equality, freedom, and patriotism.

Success

In American culture, whether one succeeds or fails is believed to be due largely to one's own efforts. We are encouraged to believe that anyone who works hard and takes advantage of opportunities can make it to the top. As there is only so much room at the top, this value may leave many people feeling as if they have failed. In midlife, many Americans redefine "success" for themselves.

Work

Most Americans believe they should work hard and laziness is generally frowned upon. We talk about people having a "work ethic" when they work hard.

Moral Concerns and Humanitarianism

Americans usually have strong opinions and tend to base their judgments on their sense of right and wrong. Americans differ, however, on the degree to which a common morality should be applied to all.

Despite their belief that individuals are responsible for their own success, Americans have a soft spot for people in need of assistance. They seem to be most generous when people are harmed by situations that they cannot control.

Efficiency

Americans stress the efficient and practical. "Saving time" is a value that drives many lives—do what you have to do in the most efficient way possible so that you will get more done.

Progress

Americans are optimists. We believe our history is one of ongoing progress. We believe that progress will make our lives better and that we can continue to improve and perfect our way of life. Some critics say that progress in the United States is blind—that we build skyscrapers, factories, and roads without any regard for their effects on the physical environment. On the other hand, the quality of people's lives in many areas has improved as a result of developments in medicine and technology. The belief in progress is closely tied to the idea that science can and eventually will overcome all natural and human-made difficulties.

Equality

"All men are created equal." This phrase from the Declaration of Independence means that the basic American value of equality has been there since the beginning of our country. Without a belief in equality and confidence of the average person, a democratic form of government would not make sense. On the other hand, by *equality* Americans mean that every individual has (or should have) equal opportunity. This ideal has not yet been realized, but we are working on it.

Freedom

Perhaps there is no greater American value than freedom. By freedom, Americans generally mean freedom from governmental controls. We believe we should be free to reach the goals we choose, speak our minds freely, associate with whom we wish, travel where we wish, and be safe from our government spying on us or taking our things unlawfully.

Patriotism

Americans are inclined to believe that the United States is a better, stronger country than all the rest, and that the American way of life is superior to all others. Patriotism implies pride in one's country and its values, but it is also closely connected to ethnocentrism.

Changing American Values

The preceding list of traditional values is not exhaustive. You might think of others you believe most Americans hold. What about consumerism? Are we a nation of consumers? Do we place a high value on having "stuff"? What do you think? Over time, new values emerge as the culture changes. Because they are new, these values are often hard to identify. However, scholars have pointed out that a new cluster of closely related values has appeared in recent years:

- Self-fulfillment.
- Narcissism.
- Hedonism.

Self-Fulfillment

Much emphasis has been placed in recent years on self-fulfillment, on the commitment to thoroughly developing one's talents and potential. Sociologist Robert Bellah says that values only have meaning if a person's "inner self" is in tune with them.

Evidence of this value of self-fulfillment is apparent in the growth of the "self-help" movement. Health clubs, diet centers, magazines, books, seminars, and web sites all challenge people to improve themselves and to experience life to its fullest. Self-help books have become big business for publishers across the country because of this new emphasis on self-improvement.

Psychologist and survey researcher Daniel Yankelovich views the shift toward self-fulfillment as positive. He believes that an emphasis on self-fulfillment will balance the ill effects that come from the traditional success value—the belief that satisfaction comes only from material gain.

Narcissism and Hedonism

Some sociologists believe that the emphasis on personal fulfillment borders on **narcissism**, or extreme self-centeredness. In "getting in tune with ourselves," we forget about others. A closely related concept is **hedonism**, or the pursuit of pleasure above all other values.

Source: Ethel Wood and Judith Lloyd Yero, *Introduction to Sociology*. Copyright © 2002 by McDougal Littell, Inc. Reprinted with permission.

 **ACTIVITY 7** Getting content from an assigned reading

Write answers to these questions about the textbook passage. When you finish, you may discuss them with your class.

1. What are values?
2. What are norms?
3. What are examples of values that are traditional in U.S. society?
4. What do critics say about the value of progress in U.S. society?
5. What is a positive aspect of the value of self-fulfillment? What is a negative aspect of this value?

ACTIVITY 8 Listening to numerical data

A survey is one of the most common research tools that sociologists use to study social groups. A survey is a research method that involves asking questions about opinions, beliefs, or behavior. The results of a survey can be expressed as numbers.

An example of a survey is the one done for the book *Global Literacies*. In this book, the authors conducted a survey of more than 1,200 business leaders from all over the world. In the survey, the leaders answered questions about their values and opinions.

Listen to a description of some of the data from the Global Literacies survey. As you listen, write in the chart what you hear.

| "Beating the competition is the highest value": Percentage of business leaders who agreed ||
Region	Percent
Europe	
Australia/New Zealand	
North America	
Asia	
Latin America	

Source: *Global Literacies: Lessons on Business Leadership and National Cultures* by Robert Rosen, Patricia Digh, Marshal Singer, and Carl Phillips. Simon and Schuster 2000.

☐ Getting Information from a Lecture: Taking Notes

The lecture you will hear in this chapter is about cultural values. As noted in Chapter 1, listening to a lecture should include:

- taking notes while the instructor is talking; your notes will help you remember what the instructor said about the material
- taking notes about course assignments

As explained in Chapters 1 through 3, a few principles or rules will help you take better notes:

- Only write content words (verbs, nouns, adjectives, and adverbs) and sometimes prepositions (such as *to*, *in*, *at*) in your notes.
- Write abbreviations for long words.
- Make your own set of easy symbols for words that are used often.
- Use a system for showing the difference between general ideas and details or examples.

Your instructor will give you some examples of sentences that you will hear in a lecture in this chapter. As you listen, take notes. Write only the important words, and use abbreviations for common words. When you finish, discuss your answers with your class. Your classmates might have good ideas about abbreviations that you can use.

Example:

Let's say that society consists of people interacting with each other as citizens of a country or members of another complex group. So a society is a complex group and inside the group there are interactions among people.

Soc: people interacting as:

cits. of count.

membs. complex group

Notice that in this example the information is given twice, in different words. This is an example of a paraphrase. In this example, the notes do not include the paraphrase of the definition. The re-statement by the speaker helps the listener understand, but it does not need to be part of the student's notes.

Notes:

1.

2.

3.

4.

5.

ACTIVITY 10   Listening to a lecture and taking notes

Now you will listen to a lecture and write notes that will help you remember what you heard.

The outline that follows has a list of important questions about the lecture you will hear. Review these questions with your class before you listen. Make sure you understand the questions, even if you do not know the answers. Then, while you are listening, try to write answers to the questions.

The outline is divided into four parts or sections. Your instructor will decide how many parts of the lecture to work with before you stop to review your notes.

When you finish this activity, you will have a good set of notes about the lecture.

Questions for Note-taking

Part 1
What is the lecture's topic?

_____

_____

What is the definition of society?

_____

_____

What is the definition of culture?

_____

_____

What is material culture?

_____

_____

What is non-material culture?

_____

_____

What are some of the parts of non-material culture?

_____

_____

Part 2

What are values?

_____

_____

What is an example of a value?

_____

_____

What are norms?

_____

_____

How do sociologists learn about the values of a culture?

_____

_____

What are some examples of values in U.S. society?

_____

_____

Part 3

What aspect of culture do business people believe they need to know about?

_____

_____

What is the topic of the book *Global Literacies*?

_____

_____

What are examples of values in Chinese society?

_____

_____

According to the author Rosen, what do business leaders need to understand?

_____

_____

Part 4

What are examples of values in Flemish culture?

_____

_____

What are examples of values in Walloon culture?

_____

_____

ACTIVITY 11 Reviewing and improving lecture notes

Work with a partner and review the notes you made on the outline in Activity 10. Discuss what you wrote. You may want to make changes in your notes after you discuss them with your partner. Then, review the textbook reading for this chapter. Use the reading to help you add information to your notes. You will use your notes later.

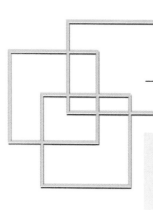

Part 2

In this section, you will work on speaking tasks that are common in academic settings. You will practice summarizing numerical information and do other work on case studies on a social science topic.

ACTIVITY 12 Summarizing numerical information

In the data below, we have the results of a survey. In this survey, 250 students were asked about the values that they think are important in work relationships. The chart shows the percentage of students who said that each of the eight values was "most important" in work relationships.

Rating of values in a group of 250 students. Percentage of students who said that each value was "most important" in work relationships	
Value	
loyalty to friends	7
respect for elders	5
honesty in communication	12
respect for authority	7
preventing others from losing face	2
egalitarianism	10
practicality	22
efficiency	35

Prepare to describe the results for each value. Use an adjective form of the value in your description. Give your descriptions to the class.

Example:

> The greatest percentage of students said that it is most important to be efficient. Thirty-five percent of the students said that efficiency was the most important value.

ACTIVITY 13 Discussing data from a survey

As you read in Part 1, a survey is one of the most common research tools that sociologists use to study social groups. This research method involves asking questions about opinions, beliefs, or behavior.

In the following table there is a summary of some data from the *Global Literacies* survey.

"Helping people adapt to change is important for leadership": Percentage of leaders who agreed	
Region	**Percent**
Europe	54
Australia/New Zealand	49
North America	44
Asia	32
Latin America	25

Master Student Tip

When you make an oral presentation, put more emphasis on content words (nouns, main verbs, adjectives, adverbs). This will make your presentation easier to understand.

Work in a small group. Discuss the survey results. What are the differences in the way the people from different countries responded? Report your discussion to the class.

Example:

> Europeans put a great deal of value on adapting to change. Fifty-four percent of leaders in Europe said that helping people adapt to change is important.

ACTIVITY 14 **Discussing case studies**

Students in a sociology class are sometimes asked to discuss a case study—a specific example of a situation—as part of their class work. In a sociology course, a case study is an example of one real-life social situation in which ideas from the course can be discussed.

Work in a group. Discuss the two case studies that follow. Report your group's answers to the class.

Case Study 1

You are a thirty-year-old manager in an international company. A sixty-year-old employee, who has worked for the company for many years, and who is below you in the company hierarchy, has made a serious mistake. The employee has lost the records of a very large order for your product. Without the records, the order cannot be completed and the company could lose thousands of dollars.

Questions

1. Imagine you are working in a culture that places a high value on loyalty, respect for age, and preventing others from losing face. How can you handle this situation based on those values?
2. Imagine you are working in a culture that places a high value on practicality, directness in communication, and efficiency. How can you handle this situation based on those values?

Case Study 2

You are an employee of an international company. Your boss has recently decided to open a new plant and to transfer half of the company's employees to the new plant. You are sure that this move is a mistake because your company does not do enough business to support the new plant. You are afraid that the move will be a disaster for the company.

Questions

1. Imagine you are working in a culture that places a high value on directness in communication, efficiency, and practicality. How can you handle this situation based on those values?
2. Imagine you are working in a culture that places a high value on loyalty, respect for authority, and preventing others from losing face. How can you handle this situation based on those values?

STRATEGY

Using Rules for Politeness

Rules for *politeness* allow speakers to show how they understand important social relationships. As a speaker of English in an academic setting, politeness rules are important to you in discussions with your classmates and teachers. It is important to use language for these purposes in a way that fits social rules in an academic setting, including rules for *preventing others from losing face.*

☐ Social Rules for Using Language: Politeness

Part of knowing a language well is knowing the social rules for using the language. Social scientists have studied the social rules for language that exist in all societies, and we know that these social rules are as important as the grammar rules that people follow to make correct sentences.

Politeness is one of the concepts that speakers need to understand to use language in a socially acceptable way. Rules for politeness allow speakers to show that they understand important social relationships. As a speaker of English in an academic setting, politeness rules are important to you in discussions with your classmates and teachers. In these situations, you may be agreeing, disagreeing, asking someone to do, or not to do something. It is important to use language for these purposes in a way that fits social rules in an academic setting.

Face

One important factor in politeness is the concept of *saving face.* Earlier in this chapter, you heard and read that face, for social scientists, is the positive image or idea that a person would like to have about himself or herself. One of the rules for speaking, in any language, is to avoid causing another person to lose face. Of course, there are many ways that speakers can help people save face or cause people to lose face, and these are different from culture to culture.

In English, speakers follow several rules to help people save face. These rules are used especially when something has happened to cause people to lose face, such as when someone has made a mistake, or when they have not carried out their obligation as a member of a group. Here are some examples of rules that can be used to help others save face when something goes wrong:

Take some of the blame

It was my fault. I should have prevented it.

Avoid criticizing

It wasn't your fault.

Assume good motivations for another person's behavior

I'm sure you didn't mean to do that.

Take the other person's point of view

You must feel bad about that.

Since everyone in society is concerned with saving face, speakers may exchange face-saving efforts:

I'm sorry; it was my fault.

No, it wasn't your fault. I should have prevented it.

Or:

I'm sorry I'm late.

I'm sure you're busy.

Status: Inequality

In English, saving face also relates to social factors such as *status*. Status is a person's position within a social group. Because of the value that many Americans, including teachers, place on egalitarianism, language learners sometimes believe that status differences are not important in academic settings. This is incorrect. For a teacher, being the leader in an academic setting is important, as well as being knowledgeable, responsible, hardworking, etc. Threats to this image threaten a teacher's face, and effective speakers know how to reduce this threat.

For example, if a student needs to remind a teacher about something important the teacher has forgotten to do, or to point out a mistake, the student can give the message while attempting to save face for the teacher.

> I'm sure you have been busy, but did you have a chance to grade my test?

Or:

> I'm not sure, but I think my answer is right. Can you explain it to me?

To threaten the face of a higher-status person, such as a teacher, would break a social rule for language. In other words, it would be *socially inappropriate* to give the same message without attempting face-saving:

> I want my test now.

Or:

> This answer is correct. You said it was incorrect.

At the same time, higher-status speakers are required to save the face of other speakers also. Often, when a person is of a higher status, the value of egalitarianism can cause that person to avoid calling attention to the difference in status. This happens even when higher-status speakers have to tell lower-status speakers what to do. Here are some rules that higher-status speakers follow to avoid calling attention to their status:

Avoid emphasizing superior status by asking questions

> When you have a chance, would you mind doing that?

Or:

> Can you bring that to me tomorrow?

Avoid emphasizing superior status by speaking indirectly

> I really would like to have that done.

Status: Equality

In general, politeness, including face-saving, is more important when there is a status difference between speakers. It is also more important when speakers do not know each other well. On the other hand, when speakers are of equal status, or if they are familiar with each other, the requirement to follow politeness rules is not so strong. For example, politeness rules are not used as much among students who are very close friends outside of class.

Losing Face

Of course, even though speakers try to save each other's face, sometimes it is not possible. Other things, such as safety or basic justice, sometimes can be more important than saving face:

> I'm sorry I'm late.
>
> Well I've been waiting for two hours! Where have you been?

> Can I help you with that?
>
> No! I'm afraid it will break!

ACTIVITY 15 **Writing a dialogue**

Work with a partner. Discuss each situation, and then write a dialogue or conversation in which each person has a role. When you write the dialogue, pay attention to the status of the speakers, and follow rules for politeness. Perform your dialogues for the class. Your instructor may want to look at your written dialogue to help you with vocabulary, grammar, and use of social rules.

Situation 1

Teacher A has given a test in a college class. The test will count as one-fourth of the total semester grade. After two weeks, the teacher has not returned the test to the class. The teacher has been away from class for a week because of sickness, and has not graded the test.

Student B is concerned about the test. The student wants to know how well she did on the test. After class, she approaches the teacher to ask for her test.

Situation 2

Student A must miss a week of class. The student must return to his or her native country to attend the wedding of an older brother. The student has already missed a week of class.

Teacher B has a rule about attendance: students who miss two weeks of class are dropped from the course, no matter what the reason is.

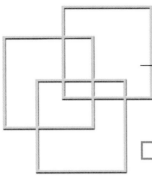

Part 3

☐ **Listening to a Short Lecture**

 ACTIVITY 16 Listening to a lecture and taking notes

Listen to the short lecture that follows. Take notes on the important points while you are listening.

While you listen, look at the "blackboard notes" that follow. These notes are examples of what an instructor might write on a blackboard to help students during class. The blackboard notes will help you follow the lecture's content, and to recognize vocabulary in the lecture. You might use the blackboard notes as part of your own notes. When you finish listening, your instructor will give you a test on the lecture's content. Your instructor may ask to see both your notes and your answers to the questions.

> Values
> Society
> Culture
>   Non-material
>   Values
> Application to business
>   Global Literacies
>   Korea protest: peaceful, orderly

☐ **Speaking about Values**

ACTIVITY 17 Reviewing notes to prepare an oral summary

Review your notes from Activity 16, and prepare to summarize the talk. Your instructor might ask you to give your oral summary in a small group or to the whole class.

ACTIVITY 18 Summarizing answers to questions

Summarize your group's answer to the questions about one of the case studies in Activity 14.

☐ Assessing Your Speaking

ACTIVITY 19 Getting feedback on your speaking skills

Your instructor may use this checklist to discuss your use of academic English in your speaking assignments.

Lecture summary	OK	Needs work	Example(s)
Content:			
▪ accurately summarized the facts			
▪ discussed values			
▪ gave appropriate examples			
Organization:			
▪ distinguished general points and examples			
Vocabulary:			
▪ used stress in academic vocabulary appropriately			
Speaking grammar:			
▪ used word forms correctly			

Case study	OK	Needs work	Example(s)
Content:			
■ accurately summarized the facts			
■ discussed values			
■ gave appropriate examples			
Organization:			
■ distinguished general points and examples			
Vocabulary:			
■ used stress in academic vocabulary appropriately			
Speaking grammar:			
■ used word forms correctly			

☐ Self-Assessment

ACTIVITY 20 Evaluating your progress

Review this list of chapter objectives. Think about your work and progress in each of these areas. Make a check mark after objectives that need your special attention in future work on academic speaking and listening.

- Recognize syllable stress in academic word families _____
- Recognize and produce word forms in a word family _____
- Take notes on important points in a lecture _____
- Summarize quantitative information from a chart _____
- Summarize a lecture's main points _____
- Use academic social rules for politeness _____

Look back at this list after you finish the work in the next chapter.

WEB POWER

You will find additional exercises related to the content in this chapter at http://esl.college.hmco.com/students.

People in White Coats Are Watching Out for You

ACADEMIC FOCUS:
BIOLOGICAL SCIENCE AND SCIENTIFIC INQUIRY

Academic Listening and Speaking Objectives

In this chapter, you will learn some of the language skills students need to do well in a science course such as biology. In part of the chapter, you will learn about listening to a formal lecture. In another part, you will learn how to prepare for a test on part of a lecture. Speaking tasks include reporting on a laboratory experiment. The lecture's topic is scientific research and human health.

Objectives are to:

- Recognize syllable stress in academic vocabulary
- Recognize and understand passive voice
- Make notes on a lecture's important points
- Work as a member of a group on an academic task
- Use adjective forms of academic vocabulary
- Summarize a laboratory investigation: describing steps in a process
- Summarize data from a chart

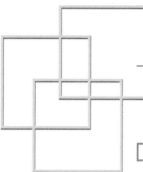

Part 1

EFFECTIVE ACADEMIC LISTENING

☐ Getting Ready for Academic Listening

ACTIVITY 1 Discussing the content of a lecture

This chapter relates to the way that science affects everyday life. To prepare for this topic, discuss the questions below.

1. Look at the label from the package of bread. The package describes the bread, the product inside, and it also gives a message to consumers about the bread. What does the package tell consumers about the bread?

This is the front of a typical package for a processed food, bread.

2. Read the label from the bread package on the next page. Do you recognize the ingredients and the additives on the list? Do you know all the names of the ingredients? Are some ingredients surprising?

Vitamin A	0%	4%		Calories	2,000	2,500
Vitamin C	0%	2%	Total fat	Less than	65g	80g
Calcium	0%	15%	Sat. Fat	Less than	20g	25g
Iron	90%	90%	Cholesterol	Less than	300g	300g
Thiamin	25%	30%	Sodium	Less than	2,400mg	2,400mg
Riboflavin	25%	35%	Potassium		3,500mg	3,500mg
Niacin	25%	25%	Total Carbohydrate		300g	375g
Vitamin B6	25%	25%			25g	30g
Folic Acid	25%	25%	Calories per gram: Fat 9 • Carbohydrate 4 • Protein 4			
Vitamin B12	25%	35%	**Ingredients:** Bleached enriched flour, water, high fructose corn			
Phosphorus	15%	25%	syrup, yeast, soybean oil. Contains 2% or less of the following:			
Magnesium	15%	20%	Wheat gluten, salt, corn flour, dough conditioners (sodium			
Zinc	10%	15%	stearoyl lactylate, vegetable mono- & diglycerides, ascorbic acid,			
Copper	10%	10%	azodicarbonamde, calcium peroxide), BHT (preservative),			
* Amount in cereal. One half cup of fat free milk			calcium sulfate, natural flavor.			
contributes an additional 40 calories, 65mg sodium,			CONTAINS WHEAT INGREDIENTS.			
6g total carbohydrate (6g sugars), and 4g protein.			**Exchange:** 2 1/2 Carbohydrates			
** Percent daily values are based on a 2,000 calorie			The dietary exchanges are based on the *Exchange Lists for*			
diet. Your daily values may be higher or lower			*Meal Planning*, ©1995 by The American Diabetes Association,			
depending on your calorie needs:			Inc. and The American Dietetic Association.			

This is an example of a label from a package of bread. The law in the United States requires manufacturers of processed food to list the nutrition value of the food, and to list the ingredients. Additives are allowed in food only if they are shown to be safe. One of the additives on this label is listed at the bottom of the label, in very small print. It is BHT, butylated hydroxytoluene. BHT is used to keep food fresh. Some scientific studies show that BHT may increase the risk of cancer. Other studies show that BHT decreases the risk of cancer.

ACTIVITY 2 Analyzing syllable-stress

Use the notation system to help you pronounce these words correctly. Your instructor will help you. (You have seen some of these words in other chapters.)

1. administration [5-4]
2. benefit [3-1]
3. design [2-2]
4. foundation [3-2]

5. link [1-1]
6. label [2-1]
7. synthetic [3-2]
8. texture [2-1]

ACTIVITY 3 Practicing word pronunciation

Listen to your instructor pronounce these words. Use the notation system to record the number of syllables and the stressed syllable. The first one is done for you. When you finish, review your answers with your instructor.

1. alternative [4 - 2]
2. chart [__ - __]
3. chemical [__ - __]
4. method [__ - __]

5. obvious [__ - __]
6. role [__ - __]
7. similar [__ - __]
8. topic [__ - __]

ACTIVITY 4   Working with academic vocabulary

Learn the meanings of the academic words used in this chapter. First, match each of the following words with the phrase that is closest to the word's meaning. Then review your answers with your class. For words you do not know, get help from your dictionary or your instructor. Use the answers for this activity to study the meanings.

1. administration _____   9. link _____

2. alternative _____   10. method _____

3. benefit _____   11. obvious _____

4. chart _____   12. role _____

5. chemical _____   13. similar _____

6. design (v.) _____   14. synthetic _____

7. foundation _____   15. texture _____

8. label _____   16. topic _____

a. writing that describes or names something

b. an organization that is created for a special purpose

c. made by people, not coming from nature

d. information organized in rows and columns

e. management

f. the kind of surface or the feeling it gives such as smooth, rough, etc.

g. the basic material things are made from

h. a different way to do something

i. job or function

j. what a talk or piece of writing is about

k. a good result

l. plan

m. way to do something

n. clear, easy to see or understand

o. connection

p. not different

POWER GRAMMAR

Passive Voice

In this chapter, you will be working with lecture material about scientific research and health. The language in the lecture has special features or qualities. Especially in a science class, we find that speakers often use *passive voice*. This is a grammar structure that speakers use when they do not want to say who or what performed an action. Here is an example. Let's imagine an instructor is talking about a scientific experiment, and says:

>   The animals were divided into two groups.

In this example, the instructor does not say who divided the animals into groups. Perhaps the instructor does not know who divided the animals; perhaps he or she does not want to think about who divided the animals, because it is not important. The instructor uses a passive sentence because it allowed him or her to avoid saying who performed the action.

We can think of this sentence as related to another sentence with the same meaning:

>   (subject)   (verb) (direct object)
>   The scientist divided the animals into two groups.

We could say that the instructor changed the sentence into a passive sentence because the subject (**the scientist**) was not necessary.

(Continued)

When we listen to passive sentences, we can recognize them by the form of the verb: it is always *be* plus a past participle.

(subject)   (verb) (direct object)
The scientist divided the animals into two groups.

(passive subject) (passive verb)
The animals were divided into two groups.

When academic listeners hear this second sentence, they understand that "someone" divided the animals into two groups.

 ACTIVITY 5 Listening for passive verb forms

Listen to these examples of passive sentences from the lecture. Write the passive verb forms that you hear. Review your answers with your class. For example, if you hear:

The mice were divided into two groups.

You write "were divided" on the line:

Example: The mice _were divided_ into two groups.

1. The ingredients _____ on the label.

2. Safe additives _____ .

3. They _____ in experiments.

4. The government _____ in the decision.

5. Many of these additives _____ .

6. Cancer research _____ on animals.

7. The experimental group _____ cyclamate.

8. The control group _____ the same way.

9. The difference _____ by the additive.

10. Cyclamate _____ by the FDA.

☐ Getting Information from a Lecture: Using Graphic Information for Academic Listening

The lecture you will hear is about the way scientists try to find answers to questions. It contains a simplified example of the type of scientific research that has a very important effect on business.

Some of the information about the research is summarized on the chart and the graph that follow. Very often, instructors present information in this form to give examples of important points in a lecture. You might see this information in a course textbook, on a blackboard drawing, or in some other visual form. This example shows the results of an experiment. The information shows the amount of cancer that resulted from adding a chemical sweetener to the food of laboratory mice. The information in the chart and the graph is the same, but it is presented in a different form.

Sweetener and cancer in mice	
Percent of sweetener in food:	**Percent of mice with cancer:**
0 (Control)	0
10	3
20	7
30	31
40	50
50	53

Sweetener and cancer in mice

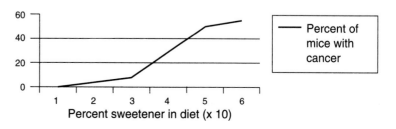

ACTIVITY **6**   Getting information from charts and graphs

Work with a partner. Study the chart and the graph. What do they show about the results of an experiment? Report what you discussed to the class.

ACTIVITY **7**   Taking lecture notes

Your instructor will give you some examples of sentences that you will hear in a lecture in this chapter. As you listen, take notes. When you finish, discuss your answers with your class. Here is an example:

Science is done in different ways by different people.

Notes:

sci. done in diff. ways by diff. people

1.

2.

3.

4.

5.

Master Student Tip

When you choose a partner or a discussion group, look for people who are different from you. You can learn new things from a classmate who has a different nationality, gender, age, or background.

ACTIVITY 8 **Taking notes on the lecture**

**Master
Student Tip**

When you take notes, do not try to write everything a speaker says; select ideas you think are important.

Now you will listen to Part 1 of the lecture and write notes to help you remember what you heard. Use the outline to take notes while you listen. Read the outline before you start to listen. Notice that in this chapter, the outline does not contain questions to help guide your note-taking.

Review your notes about Part 1 with a classmate. Exchange ideas about good ways to take notes on this part. Then review your answers with the whole class.

Part 1

The main topic of the lecture:

_____

_____

_____

Food additives are:

_____

_____

_____

_____

Examples of government groups that test the safety of food:

_____

_____

_____

_____

Ways that people decide what is true in everyday life:

_____

_____

_____

_____

Using Review to Prepare for a Test

Instructors often help students prepare for tests in class. One kind
of preparation is a review of topics that will be on a test. In this kind
of review, the instructor lists the topics that will be tested, and gives
details about what the students are supposed to know. Understanding
an instructor's review for a test helps you save time and energy when
you study for tests.

ACTIVITY 9 Taking notes on the lecture

*Listen to Part 2 of the lecture, and again take notes. Part 2 contains more
details than Part 1, and your notes should reflect this. Review your notes
about Part 2 with a classmate. Exchange ideas about good ways to take notes
on this part of the lecture. Then review your answers with the whole class.*

Part 2

The three steps in the scientific method are:

Make _____

Develop _____

Test _____

Steps used in studying the effect of cyclamate:

_____

_____

_____

_____

Results of experiment:

_____

_____

_____

Conclusion of experiment:

_____

_____

_____

_____

_____

Results of this research for business:

_____

_____

_____

_____

_____

What consumer groups say about additives:

_____

_____

_____

_____

What manufacturers say about food additives:

_____

_____

_____

_____

Advice from nutrition experts:

_____

_____

_____

_____

☐ Preparing for a Lecture Test

Instructors often help students prepare for tests. One kind of preparation is a *review* of topics that will be on a test. In this type of review, the instructor lists the topics, and gives details about what the students are supposed to know for the test. Understanding an instructor's review can be very important as it can help students save time and energy when they study for tests. Instructors and students often use the following vocabulary in reviewing for a test. Some of these words have a special meaning when used in this way.

Cover:

To explain or discuss in class; when an instructor *covers* a topic, it means students are expected to know about this topic.

> **Example:**

> We covered the main structures of the nervous system last week.

Review:

To give information a second time; sometimes this means to clarify topics through more explanation.

> **Example:**

> Let's review the main causes of heart disease.

Go over:

To cover or to review; this can mean to discuss in a general way, either for the first time ("cover") or a second time ("review").

> **Examples:**

> We went over the circulatory system two weeks ago. (cover)

> Today we'll go over the topics from chapter two. (review)

☐ Listening for Important Information

Instructors use special language to identify important information for a test. Sometimes they use polite request or "command" forms of verbs to tell students what to learn. Here are examples:

You'll need to know _____.

You should know _____.

I want you to know _____.

I'd like you to know _____.

Know _____.

Just as important, instructors also tell students what is not important for a test. Understanding this information can save time for students. Here are examples:

You don't need to know _____.

Don't worry about _____.

 ACTIVITY 🔟 **Preparing for a test on a lecture**

Students use information from a review session to prepare for tests. After a review session, a student should be able to guess the questions that will appear on the test. The review session reminds students what the teacher thinks is important.

You will listen to an example of a review session. Look at the chart on page 134, which summarizes information about several food additives. The information on the chart was mentioned in the short lecture you heard. Prepare for a test on this chart. While listening to the review session, make notes on the chart showing which information will be on the test.

After listening to the review session, answer the questions. Your instructor will review the answers with the class.

Additive	Use	Example of food	Reported side effects or health concerns
Aspartame	sweetener	NutraSweet	dizziness, headaches, brain damage
Saccharin	sweetener	sweeteners	cancer in lab animals
Caffeine	stimulant	soft drinks	ulcers, insomnia, birth defects
MSG	improve flavor	prepared foods	headaches, burning sensation on skin
Nitrate and nitrite	preservative	processed meat	forms a carcinogen
BHA, BHT	preservative	cereal	cancer
Sulfites	preserve color	salads, dried fruit	hives, death
Red Dye No. 3	color	maraschino cherries	thyroid cancer in lab animals

Questions

Be prepared to explain your answer.

1. Could the test include questions about the scientific method?

2. Could the test include questions about the health effects of additives?

3. Could the test ask for examples of a food that contains a preservative?

4. Could the test ask about the reason for putting additives in food?

5. Based on the review, which of these questions would you expect to see on the test? (You do not need to answer the questions; only decide if they will be on the test.)

   a. Give an example of a food additive that is used to change the color of food.

   b. Give an example of a food that contains caffeine.

   c. What are the possible health effects of BHT?

   d. Why are sulfates added to foods?

   e. What is an example of a food that contains Red Dye Number 3?

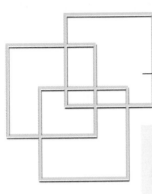

Part 2

In this section, you will work on academic speaking tasks that are common in science classes: reporting on a laboratory experiment and summarizing research data. For both these tasks it will help you to know different forms of the academic words that you use.

☐ Word Forms: Adjectives Ending in *-ical*

The following list shows noun forms of Academic Word List words you have seen before in this book, along with an adjective form of the same word. Notice that the adjective forms end with *-ical*, one of the common adjective endings for academic words. Also notice the pattern in the stressed syllable for each adjective form. In these words, the main or primary stress is on the syllable that comes before *-ical*.

Noun Form		Adjective Form with *-ical*	
economy	[4-2]	economical	[5-3]
hierarchy	[3-1]	hierarchical	[5-3]
hypothesis	[4-2]	hypothetical	[5-3]
period	[3-1]	periodical	[5-3]
philosophy	[4-2]	philosophical	[5-3]
psychology	[4-2]	psychological	[5-3]
sociology	[5-3]	sociological	[6-4]

The words that end with *-ical* generally have the same stress pattern. When you see one of these words that is new to you, you can assume that the main stress is on the syllable before *-ical*. For example, *neurology* is the study of the nervous system, including the brain. The adjective form for this word is *neurological*. You can guess that the stress is on the third syllable.

ACTIVITY 11 Using academic vocabulary in a discussion

Work with a partner. Read the sentences and questions that follow. Take turns answering the questions using an adjective form of the AWL word. (Use the words listed above.) Make sure each answer is in the form of a sentence.

1. The discussion was related to groups of people in a culture. What kind of discussion was it?
2. It was a system in which there was a person at the top and other people at the bottom. What kind of system was it?
3. The event happened after a certain amount of time. What kind of event was it?
4. Their disagreement was about basic ideas and beliefs. What kind of disagreement did they have?
5. The problem was related to human behavior and thoughts. What kind of problem was it?
6. It was a preliminary idea or guess about how things work. What kind of idea was it?

☐ Performing a Simple Experiment

Students in science courses participate in laboratory ("lab") work, in which they conduct physical tests or study materials or objects. For example, students in a chemistry course study chemical reactions, and in a biology course observe examples of a biological process or principle. Labs almost always involve groups of students. Participating in lab groups requires a special kind of language ability.

In this section, you will participate in a simple lab group, and your group reporter will report the results of your work to the class. The language for participating in this simple lab is the same language you will need to participate in a real lab. Before you carry out the lab, read all the directions to make sure you understand the steps.

ACTIVITY 12 Talking about the effect of mind control

Some people believe the mind can be used to affect everyday physical events. For example, people may believe they can wish for something to happen, and their wish, which is a kind of thought, can have an effect on an event. We can observe people trying to use their minds to affect the result of sporting events, games, etc. Sometimes the word *psychokenesis* is used to describe the attempt to use the mind to move physical objects. We can test the effect of this kind of "mind power" by a simple experiment.

Before you begin, review the steps in an experiment from your notes on Activity 9. Make sure you understand the terms *hypothesis, control treatment, experimental treatment, results,* and *conclusion.*

Part A. Hypothesis

As a group, make a prediction about a person's ability to use his or her mind to cause a coin to land on the "heads" side. Your hypothesis might be that a person can cause this to happen, or that a person cannot cause this to happen.

Part B. Procedure: control treatment

Determine the number of times a coin will land "heads" (with the head up) or "tails" (with the head down) without any other influence besides flipping in the air.

1. *Select any coin from the pocket or purse of a group member.*
2. *Have a group member flip the coin in the air, catch it without looking at it, and place it on the back of his or her hand. Record whether the face or head is up ("heads") or down ("tails"). Repeat this fifty times. Record the number of times the coin landed "tails" or "heads."*
3. *Calculate the percentage of flips that resulted in "heads" or "tails."*

Part C. Procedure: experimental treatment

Determine the number of times a coin will land "heads" or "tails" when a group member attempts to use his or her mind to cause the coin to land "heads" up.

1. *Use the same coin used in Part 1.*
2. *Have the same group member flip the coin. During the flip, have one group member attempt to affect the result of the coin flip. This person should not touch the coin, but should only observe the coin flip. Have the observer attempt to cause the coin to land "heads" up. This might include thinking about "heads," talking to the coin, etc. Repeat this fifty times. Record the number of times the coin landed "tails" or "heads."*
3. *Calculate the percentage of flips that resulted in "heads" or "tails."*

Part D. Results

Compare the percentage of flips that resulted in "heads" in each treatment.

Part E. Conclusion

Describe the meaning of the results. Does this experiment show something about the power of "mind control"? What explains the results of the experiment? Here are some possible conclusions to think about; you may agree or disagree with them.

- The observer was able to change the result by mind control.
- There were more "heads" in the experimental treatment, but this was not caused by mind control.
- The observer was not able to change the result by mind control.
- The observer was not able to use mind control to affect the result, but other people might be able to do it.
- It is possible that another observer was affecting the result in some way.
- It is possible that the person who flipped the coin affected the result in some way.

ACTIVITY 13 **Making an oral laboratory report**

Your group will work together to create an oral report about the "mind control" experiment. Group members will help the reporter make notes for the report. (See a description of the reporter's role on page 25.)
The report should describe the experiment's purpose, and include the hypothesis, a description of the procedures (both the experimental treatment and the control treatments), the results of the experiment, and the group's conclusion.

Here is an outline that your group may want to use to prepare notes for your report on the experiment.

Purpose of experiment: To test _____

Hypothesis: That an observer's mind (can / cannot) affect the number of times a coin flip results in "heads."

Procedure: control treatment:

_____

_____

_____

_____

Procedure: experimental treatment:

_____

_____

_____

_____

Results: the effect of the attempt to use mind control:

_____

_____

_____

_____

Conclusion: The experiment (shows / doesn't show) that the hypothesis might be (right / wrong) because:

_____

_____

_____

_____

_____

_____

_____

_____

_____

_____

_____

_____

_____

_____

_____

_____

_____

_____

_____

_____

In a report on an experiment, the passive voice is often used. This is because the emphasis in the report is on the action, and not on the person doing the action. (You may wish to review passive voice forms with your instructor before you work in this speaking task.)

Here is an example of part of a report on this experiment.

> . . . The purpose of the experiment was to test the effect of mind control on the flipping of a coin. The experiment was designed to attempt to use mind control to cause a coin to land on "heads."
>
> The first part of the experiment was the control treatment. In this part, there was no attempt to use mind control. A coin was selected from the pocket of a group member. It was flipped fifty times, and the number of "heads" was counted . . .

ACTIVITY 14 Summarizing data from a chart

Look at the chart about food additives and your notes from the lecture. (See page 134.) Describe the uses and possible health effects of three of the additives on the chart.

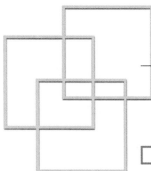

Part 3

ASSESSING YOUR ACADEMIC LISTENING AND SPEAKING SKILLS

☐ Listening to a Short Lecture

 ACTIVITY 15 Listening to a lecture and taking notes

Listen to the short lecture on science that follows. While you listen, take notes on the important points. Look at the "blackboard notes" while you listen. They will help you follow the content of the lecture.

Controlled experiments on additives:

Study about:
    Additives in the diet
Experimental treatment:
    A group of animals or
    people who have the
    additive in their diet ➤ More health problems ➤ Additive is not safe?
Control treatment:
    A group of animals
    or people who do
    not have the
    additive in their diet ➤ Fewer health problems
Tartrazine: food coloring

Study by British Nutritional Foundation

ACTIVITY 16 Using lecture notes to prepare for a test

After you listen to the short lecture, study your notes. Work in a small group and prepare for a test on the lecture. In your group, make a list of questions you might expect to see on the test. Discuss answers to these questions in your group. Your instructor will ask you to report your questions and answers to the whole class.

Your instructor will give you a test on the content of the lecture. Your instructor may ask to see your notes as well as your answers to the questions.

ACTIVITY 17 Preparing two short oral summaries

1. *Imagine that a classmate asked you for a summary of the short lecture on page 143 as a review. Review your notes. Prepare to summarize the talk. Your instructor might ask you to give your oral summary in a small group or to the whole class.*

2. *Look at the chart and graph from the experiment about the sweetener and cancer, and your lecture notes. (See pages 127 and 129–131.) Describe the procedure and results of the experiment.*

☐ Assessing Your Speaking

ACTIVITY 18 **Getting feedback on your speaking skills**

Your instructor may use this checklist to let you know about your use of academic English in your speaking assignments.

1. Summary of the lecture	OK	Needs work	Example(s)
Content:			
▪ accurately summarized the lecture			
▪ gave appropriate examples			
Organization:			
▪ explained steps in the procedure and conclusion of an experiment			
Vocabulary:			
▪ used stress in academic vocabulary appropriately			
Speaking grammar:			
▪ used passive structures correctly			

2. Summary of the data on sweetener and cancer	OK	Needs work	Example(s)
Content:			
■ accurately summarized the chart or graph			
■ gave appropriate examples			
Organization:			
Vocabulary:			
■ used stress in academic vocabulary appropriately			
Speaking grammar:			
■ used passive structures correctly			

☐ Self-Assessment

ACTIVITY 19 **Evaluating your progress**

Review this list of chapter objectives. Think about your work and progress in each of these areas. Make a check mark after objectives that need your special attention in future work on academic speaking and listening.

- ▪ Recognize syllable stress in academic vocabulary _____

- ▪ Recognize and understand passive voice _____

- ▪ Make notes on a lecture's important points _____

- ▪ Work as a member of a group on an academic task _____

- ▪ Use adjective forms of academic vocabulary _____

- ▪ Summarize a laboratory investigation: describing steps in a

  process _____

- ▪ Summarize data from a chart _____

Look back at this list after you finish with the work in the next chapter.

WEB POWER

You will find additional exercises related to the content in this chapter at http://esl.college.hmco.com/students.

6

Is It Love, or Is It Money?

ACADEMIC FOCUS: LITERATURE

Academic Listening and Speaking Objectives

In this chapter, you will learn some of the language skills that are important in discussing literature. In part of the chapter, you will learn about listening to an explanation about an assignment. In another part, you will learn about discussing your ideas with classmates. The topic of the talk in this chapter is writing a persuasive paper about issues in literature.

Objectives are to:

- Recognize syllable stress in academic vocabulary
- Take notes on a class handout
- Understand paraphrases
- Respond to arguments: agreeing and disagreeing
- Persuade an audience about issues, claims, and evidence

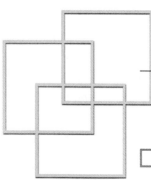

Part 1

EFFECTIVE ACADEMIC LISTENING

☐ Getting Ready for Academic Listening

Master Student Tip

Don't always fill the same role in discussion groups; the challenging roles can help improve your communication skills.

ACTIVITY 1 Discussing literature

This chapter is about literature, which is writing as an art form. Discuss these questions in a group. One group member should act as a reporter, and report your answers to the class.

What is your experience with reading literature? Have you studied literature in your first language? In English? Do you read literature for enjoyment? Have you read literature as part of your school work? Do you have a favorite author or favorite books?

ACTIVITY 2 Analyzing syllable-stress in new vocabulary

The words that follow are important in the talk you will hear. Some of them may be new to you. Most are from the Academic Word List. Find the words in your dictionary, become familiar with their meanings, and be prepared to pronounce them correctly. Use the system for noting the number of syllables and the stressed syllables that you learned in Chapter 1 (page 5). Your instructor may ask you to pronounce these words before you do the other work in this chapter.

1. assign	[___ - ___]		6. issue	[___ - ___]
2. context	[___ - ___]		7. obvious	[___ - ___]
3. culture	[___ - ___]		8. summary	[___ - ___]
4. define	[___ - ___]		9. text	[___ - ___]
5. identified	[___ - ___]		10. thesis	[___ - ___]

ACTIVITY 3 **Practicing word pronunciation**

Listen to your instructor pronounce these words. Use the notation system to record the number of syllables and the stressed syllable. When you finish, review your answers with your instructor.

1. assignment   [—— - ——]   6. obviously   [—— - ——]

2. definition   [—— - ——]   7. physical   [—— - ——]

3. evidence   [—— - ——]   8. policy   [—— - ——]

4. focus   [—— - ——]   9. process   [—— - ——]

5. logic   [—— - ——]   10. summarize   [—— - ——]

ACTIVITY 4 **Working with academic vocabulary**

Learn or review the meanings of the academic words used in this chapter. Write the meanings in your own words. Make notes about all the forms of the word that you know. Use a dictionary for words that you do not know.

assign

_____

_____

_____

_____

culture

_____

_____

_____

_____

define

_____

_____

_____

_____

evidence

_____

_____

_____

_____

identify

_____

_____

_____

_____

focus

_____

_____

_____

_____

issue

_____

_____

_____

_____

logic

_____

_____

_____

_____

obvious

_____

_____

_____

_____

physical

_____

_____

_____

_____

policy

_____

_____

_____

_____

process

_____

_____

_____

_____

summarize

_____

_____

_____

_____

text

_____

_____

_____

_____

thesis

_____

_____

_____

_____

ACTIVITY 5 Listening for and pronouncing vocabulary

Listen to your instructor read each of these sentences. Write the missing words in the blanks. One word is from the vocabulary lists above. After you finish, read aloud what you wrote.

1. I'd like to explain how to do your _____.

2. It's just a _____ about persuasion in your textbook.

3. So let's take a look at this handout and I'll explain the different

    _____.

4. Writing a persuasive paper _____ on what you're

    reading.

5. You're going to _____, or an important question about

    the text.

6. There's no point doing a lot of work to think _____.

7. It could be an issue of social or _____, a question

    about the society of a certain time or place.

8. An issue _____ is a question about how society

    should be.

☐ Using a Text to Prepare for a Discussion

This chapter's activities relate to the short story "The Gift of the Magi" by O. Henry. This story was written about one hundred years ago, but the issues in the story are still important to people today. Many O. Henry stories are about the lives of ordinary people, and they are famous for having a "twist" or surprise at the end.

ACTIVITY 6   **Using your textbook to prepare for a lecture**

Read the following passage from a history textbook. Take notes about important ideas, events, or details in the passage, and use a dictionary to find out the meaning of words that interest you. (You do not need to know many of the unusual words used in this passage.)

THE GIFT OF THE MAGI

1   One dollar and eighty-seven cents. That was all. And sixty cents of it was in pennies. Pennies saved one and two at a time by bulldozing[1] the grocer and the vegetable man and the butcher until one's cheeks burned with the silent imputation of parsimony[2] that such close dealing implied. Three times Della counted it. One dollar and eighty-seven cents. And the next day would be Christmas.

2   There was clearly nothing to do but flop down on the shabby little couch and howl. So Della did it. Which instigates the moral reflection that life is made up of sobs, sniffles, and smiles, with sniffles predominating.[3]

1. *bulldozing* = puting pressure on
2. *parsimony* = being too careful with money
3. *sniffles* = here, less sad than sobs, but not as happy as smiles

3   While the mistress of the home is gradually subsiding from the first stage to the second,[4] take a look at the home. A furnished flat at $8 per week. It did not exactly beggar description, but it certainly had that word on the lookout for the mendicancy squad.[5]

4   In the vestibule[6] below was a letter-box into which no letter would go, and an electric button from which no mortal finger could coax a ring. Also appertaining thereunto was a card bearing the name "Mr. James Dillingham Young."

5   The "Dillingham" had been flung to the breeze during a former period of prosperity when its possessor was being paid $30 per week. Now, when the income was shrunk to $20,[7] though, they were thinking seriously of contracting to a modest and unassuming D. But whenever Mr. James Dillingham Young came home and reached his flat above he was called "Jim" and greatly hugged by Mrs. James Dillingham Young, already introduced to you as Della. Which is all very good.

6   Della finished her cry and attended to her cheeks with the powder rag. She stood by the window and looked out dully at a gray cat walking a gray fence in a gray backyard. Tomorrow would be Christmas Day, and she had only $1.87 with which to buy Jim a present. She had been saving every penny she could for months, with this result. Twenty dollars a week doesn't go far. Expenses had been greater than she had calculated. They always are. Only $1.87 to buy a present for Jim. Her Jim. Many a happy hour she had spent planning for something nice for him. Something fine and rare and sterling—something just a little bit near to being worthy of the honor of being owned by Jim.

7   There was a pier-glass[8] between the windows of the room. Perhaps you have seen a pier-glass in an $8 flat. A very thin and very agile person may, by observing his reflection in a rapid sequence of longitudinal strips, obtain a fairly accurate conception of his looks. Della, being slender, had mastered the art.

8   Suddenly she whirled from the window and stood before the glass. Her eyes were shining brilliantly, but her face had lost its color within twenty seconds. Rapidly she pulled down her hair and let it fall to its full length.

4. that is, going from sobs to sniffles
5. the apartment was very poor-looking
6. *vestibule* = entrance
7. $20 a week at the time of the story, would be about $80 a week, or about $16,000 a year
8. *pier-glass* = a kind of mirror

9   Now, there were two possessions of the James Dillingham Youngs in which they both took a mighty pride. One was Jim's gold watch that had been his father's and his grandfather's. The other was Della's hair. Had the queen of Sheba[9] lived in the flat across the airshaft, Della would have let her hair hang out the window some day to dry just to depreciate Her Majesty's jewels and gifts. Had King Solomon[10] been the janitor, with all his treasures piled up in the basement, Jim would have pulled out his watch every time he passed, just to see him pluck at his beard from envy.

10   So now Della's beautiful hair fell about her rippling and shining like a cascade of brown waters. It reached below her knee and made itself almost a garment for her. And then she did it up again nervously and quickly. Once she faltered for a minute and stood still while a tear or two splashed on the worn red carpet.

11   On went her old brown jacket; on went her old brown hat. With a whirl of skirts and with the brilliant sparkle still in her eyes, she fluttered out the door and down the stairs to the street.

12   Where she stopped the sign read: "Mme. Sofronie. Hair Goods of All Kinds." One flight up Della ran, and collected herself, panting. Madame, large, too white, chilly, hardly looked the "Sofronie."[11]

13   "Will you buy my hair?" asked Della.

14   "I buy hair," said Madame. "Take yer hat off and let's have a sight at the looks of it."

15   Down rippled the brown cascade.

16   "Twenty dollars," said Madame, lifting the mass with a practised hand.

17   "Give it to me quick," said Della.

18   Oh, and the next two hours tripped by on rosy wings. Forget the hashed metaphor.[12] She was ransacking the stores for Jim's present.

9. *the queen of Sheba* = a fantastically rich woman
10. *King Solomon* = a fantastically rich man
11. as though Mme. Sofronie wants people to think she is French, but she really is not
12. The author first says that time danced on its wings, and then makes a joke about his bad comparison.

19   She found it at last. It surely had been made for Jim and no one else. There was no other like it in any of the stores, and she had turned all of them inside out. It was a platinum fob chain simple and chaste in design, properly proclaiming its value by substance alone and not by meretricious ornamentation—as all good things should do.[13] It was even worthy of The Watch. As soon as she saw it she knew that it must be Jim's. It was like him. Quietness and value—the description applied to both. Twenty-one dollars they took from her for it, and she hurried home with the 87 cents. With that chain on his watch Jim might be properly anxious about the time in any company. Grand as the watch was, he sometimes looked at it on the sly on account of the old leather strap that he used in place of a chain.

20   When Della reached home her intoxication gave way a little to prudence and reason. She got out her curling irons and lighted the gas and went to work repairing the ravages made by generosity added to love. Which is always a tremendous task, dear friends— a mammoth task.

21   Within forty minutes her head was covered with tiny, close-lying curls that made her look wonderfully like a truant schoolboy. She looked at her reflection in the mirror long, carefully, and critically.

22   "If Jim doesn't kill me," she said to herself, "before he takes a second look at me, he'll say I look like a Coney Island chorus girl.[14] But what could I do—oh! what could I do with a dollar and eighty-seven cents?"

23   At 7 o'clock the coffee was made and the frying-pan was on the back of the stove hot and ready to cook the chops.

24   Jim was never late. Della doubled the fob chain in her hand and sat on the corner of the table near the door that he always entered. Then she heard his step on the stair away down on the first flight, and she turned white for just a moment. She had a habit for saying little silent prayers about the simplest everyday things, and now she whispered: "Please God, make him think I am still pretty."

13. The chain's quality was because it was made of good material, not because it was fancy.
14. *Coney Island chorus girl* = a singer in an inexpensive show

25   The door opened and Jim stepped in and closed it. He looked thin and very serious. Poor fellow, he was only twenty-two—and to be burdened with a family! He needed a new overcoat and he was without gloves.

26   Jim stopped inside the door, as immovable as a setter at the scent of quail.[15] His eyes were fixed upon Della, and there was an expression in them that she could not read, and it terrified her. It was not anger, nor surprise, nor disapproval, nor horror, nor any of the sentiments that she had been prepared for. He simply stared at her fixedly with that peculiar expression on his face.

27   Della wriggled off the table and went for him.

28   "Jim, darling," she cried, "don't look at me that way. I had my hair cut off and sold because I couldn't have lived through Christmas without giving you a present. It'll grow out again—you won't mind, will you? I just had to do it. My hair grows awfully fast. Say 'Merry Christmas!' Jim, and let's be happy. You don't know what a nice—what a beautiful, nice gift I've got for you."

29   "You've cut off your hair?" asked Jim, laboriously, as if he had not arrived at that patent fact yet even after the hardest mental labor.

30   "Cut it off and sold it," said Della. "Don't you like me just as well, anyhow? I'm me without my hair, ain't I?"

31   Jim looked about the room curiously.

32   "You say your hair is gone?" he said, with an air almost of idiocy.

33   "You needn't look for it," said Della. "It's sold, I tell you—sold and gone, too. It's Christmas Eve, boy. Be good to me, for it went for you. Maybe the hairs of my head were numbered," she went on with sudden serious sweetness, "but nobody could ever count my love for you. Shall I put the chops on, Jim?"

34   Out of his trance Jim seemed quickly to wake. He enfolded his Della. For ten seconds let us regard with discreet scrutiny some inconsequential object in the other direction. Eight dollars a week or a million a year—what is the difference? A mathematician or a wit would give you the wrong answer. The magi brought valuable gifts,[16] but that was not among them. This dark assertion will be illuminated later on.

15. like a hunting dog concentrating on a bird
16. The magi were the kings who brought gifts to Jesus in the story of Christmas. According to the story they were wise men.

35   Jim drew a package from his overcoat pocket and threw it upon the table.

36   "Don't make any mistake, Dell," he said, "about me. I don't think there's anything in the way of a haircut or a shave or a shampoo that could make me like my girl any less. But if you'll unwrap that package you may see why you had me going a while at first."

37   White fingers and nimble tore at the string and paper. And then an ecstatic scream of joy; and then, alas! a quick feminine change to hysterical tears and wails, necessitating the immediate employment of all the comforting powers of the lord of the flat.

38   For there lay The Combs—the set of combs, side and back, that Della had worshipped long in a Broadway window. Beautiful combs, pure tortoise shell, with jewelled rims—just the shade to wear in the beautiful vanished hair. They were expensive combs, she knew, and her heart had simply craved and yearned over them without the least hope of possession. And now, they were hers, but the tresses[17] that should have adorned the coveted adornments[18] were gone.

39   But she hugged them to her bosom, and at length she was able to look up with dim eyes and a smile and say: "My hair grows so fast, Jim!"

40   And then Della leaped up like a little singed cat and cried, "Oh, oh!"

41   Jim had not yet seen his beautiful present. She held it out to him eagerly upon her open palm. The dull precious metal seemed to flash with a reflection of her bright and ardent spirit.

42   "Isn't it a dandy, Jim? I hunted all over town to find it. You'll have to look at the time a hundred times a day now. Give me your watch. I want to see how it looks on it."

43   Instead of obeying, Jim tumbled down on the couch and put his hands under the back of his head and smiled.

44   "Dell," said he, "let's put our Christmas presents away and keep 'em a while. They're too nice to use just at present. I sold the watch to get the money to buy your combs. And now suppose you put the chops on."

17. *tresses* = long hair
18. *coveted adornments* = the decoration that she really had wanted

45   The magi, as you know, were wise men—wonderfully wise men—who brought gifts to the Babe in the manger.[19] They invented the art of giving Christmas presents. Being wise, their gifts were no doubt wise ones, possibly bearing the privilege of exchange in case of duplication. And here I have lamely related to you the uneventful chronicle of two foolish children in a flat who most unwisely sacrificed for each other the greatest treasures of their house. But in a last word to the wise of these days let it be said that of all who give gifts these two were the wisest. Of all who give and receive gifts, such as they are wisest. Everywhere they are wisest. They are the magi.

ACTIVITY 7 Getting content from an assigned reading

Answer these questions about the short story. Discuss your answers with your class.

1. The story shows us how poor Jim and Della are. What are some details that show that they are poor?
2. What are Jim and Della's treasures? Why do you think they are so important to them?
3. Near the end of the story we find out why Jim acts so strangely when he comes home and sees Della. Why does he act so strangely?
4. At the end of the story, the author tells us that Jim and Della are very wise, even though they seem to have made a mistake. Why does he say they are wise?

19. According to the story of the first Christmas, they gave presents to Jesus, who was born in a manger, or a stable.

STRATEGY

Making Notes on a Handout

Instructors often give written descriptions of complex assignments on a handout. In reviewing a handout, instructors very often give paraphrases of the instructions and give examples of any topics that are not clear. If you add your own notes to the written instructions, it will be easier to do the assignment according to the instructor's standards.

☐ Getting Information from a Talk: Taking Notes on a Handout

The talk you will hear in this chapter is about making persuasive arguments about a piece of literature. In this case, the talk is about how to complete an assignment related to a literature course.

This talk is different from other lectures in this textbook because it is a detailed explanation about how to do an assignment. The talk is connected to a paper— a "handout,"—that the teacher has given the students. The students' job in this talk is to follow the handout as the teacher explains the steps in doing the work.

The handout is on page 162.

Lit I
Prof. Joyce
Spring semester
Writing a Persuasive Paper in Response to Literature
Persuasion is not: a fight with winners and losers
Writing a persuasive paper does help in reading and responding to literature:

> it gives a purpose for reading
>
> it gives direction for our thoughts about what we read
>
> it gives readers a chance to think critically

Steps

1. State an **issue**. An issue is a question with "no obvious, immediate answer." As we read, issues come to mind.
   For instance, an issue might be a question about a **definition**. We might ask how a word used in the literature is defined: "What does *wise* mean?" "What is *love*?"
     Another example of an issue might be of **cause and effect**: "Why did Della decide to give up her treasure?"
     Another example might be of **social policy**: "Does the story try to show that the poor are happy?"

2. Make a **claim** about an issue. A claim is "a statement that is made in the hope that it will be considered true." For example, we might claim that:
   In "The Gift of the Magi" the word *wise* means being ready to give up material things for love."
   Or:
   "Della gave up her one treasure because she valued Jim's happiness more than her own."
     When you state a claim about an issue, you have written a **thesis statement** for your persuasive paper, a statement of the paper's main or central idea.

3. **Persuade** your audience about your claim. When you persuade, you must **consider your audience**, that is, make an argument that considers what you know about the people who are reading or listening to what you say. Also, you must **provide evidence**, that is, observations or facts that support your claim.
     Appeals are the heart of persuasion: when we try to persuade, we think of how to present claims so that the audience will accept them. Examples are appeals to reason, to ethical beliefs, to emotions.

☐ Recognizing Language for Academic Listening: Paraphrases of Terms

This chapter's speaker helps students follow her talk by *paraphrasing*, or repeating an explanation with different words. It is important to recognize paraphrases in academic speech, since they are designed to help listeners focus on the important ideas in a talk or lecture.

Here is an example of a paraphrase in the text:

> I believe that this kind of writing is helpful when you study literature because it gives you a *purpose* for reading. In other words, it can give you a job to do while you read.

In this example, the speaker is paraphrasing the phrase "gives you a purpose for reading." The paraphrase is introduced with "in other words." The paraphrase is "can give you a job to do while you read." This paraphrase is intended to be helpful to students, because it allows the teacher two chances to give the same message, and it allows students to hear two ways to express the same idea. Although the paraphrase helps in understanding, students do not need to write the same information twice in their notes.

Here are other examples of paraphrases:

> Also, writing a persuasive paper helps give you direction while you are reading a text. It focuses your attention on what you're reading.

> The last step is to persuade your reader that your claim is true. You try to give evidence, or factual information, that shows that your claim is true.

In some cases, a paraphrase allows the instructor to add more information to an explanation.

Example:

> Part of what you do is to consider your audience. That means that you think about your reader, what they might know or not know about your issue and what they might think about your issue.

In this example, the instructor paraphrases "consider your audience" and also gives information about what writers should consider or think about.

🎧 **ACTIVITY 8** **Paraphrasing**

Listen to these three examples of paraphrasing from the talk for this chapter. Make notes on the paraphrase of each of these phrases. In other words, write the words that the speaker uses to explain the meaning of each of these phrases.

Here is an example. You hear:

You're going to state an issue, or an important question about the text.

You write:

an issue:

an important question

1. make a claim:

   _____

   _____

   the three main steps:

   _____

   _____

   _____

2. a claim:

   _____

   _____

3. not obvious:

   _____

   _____

ACTIVITY 9 **Listening to a lecture and taking notes**

Now you will hear the talk. The talk's purpose is to explain how to write a persuasive paper. As you listen, take notes on the handout on page 162. When you take notes, write things that will help you to better understand the topic: making a persuasive argument about literature. As with any notes, write only the important words, and use abbreviations for common words.

Here is an example of note-taking on the handout during the teacher's talk. The handout says:

> Making a persuasive argument **does** help in reading and responding to literature:
>
> purpose for reading
>
> direction

While reviewing this part of the handout, the instructor says:

> I believe that this kind of writing is helpful when you study literature because it gives you a *purpose* for reading. In other words, it can give you a job to do while you read. Also, writing a persuasive paper helps give you direction while you are reading a text. It focuses your attention on what you're reading. I think that makes reading more meaningful and more fun.

You can add some notes to the handout that help explain the written words, like this example:

> Making a persuasive argument **does** help in reading and responding to literature:
>
> purpose for reading—*Give a job to do*
>
> direction—*Focus attn.; more meaningful, fun*

ACTIVITY 10 **Reviewing and improving lecture notes**

Work with a partner and review the notes you made on the handout in Activity 9. Discuss what you wrote. You may want to make changes in your notes after you discuss them with your partner. When you finish, put your notes aside. You will use them later.

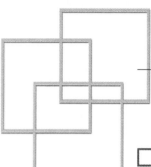

Part 2

EFFECTIVE ACADEMIC SPEAKING

☐ **Speaking about a Writing Assignment**

In the activities that follow, you will practice discussing ideas about the short story you read. Although you will not be asked to write a composition, you will be asked to do some speaking tasks to prepare you to write a persuasive paper. These tasks include making a claim about a piece of literature, and providing evidence to support the claim. The style of a discussion about these topics is less formal than the style used in writing. The following are some claims that can be made in discussing the Gift of the Magi.

- Love is more important in a relationship than money.
- Della and Jim's relationship will succeed because they are "wise."
- Della and Jim can never be happy because they are poor.
- Jim and Della are happy because each thinks of the other before himself or herself.

Evidence in the story

Some evidence to help support these claims might be found in the story. For example, if we want evidence to show that Jim and Della are poor, we can find the following evidence:

- their doorbell does not work
- there is no mail in the mailbox
- Jim needs a new overcoat
- the apartment has a cheap mirror
- Della can only save $1.87
- Jim is thin

If we look for evidence to show that Jim and Della think of each other before themselves, we can find that:

- Della sells her most important possession for Jim
- Jim sells his most important possession for Della
- Della worries how her short hair will affect Jim
- Jim is afraid that Della cannot use his gift

We can also look for evidence outside of the story.

Evidence about marriage, poverty, and happiness

Sociologists have studied how to measure people's feelings of happiness, and have studied the connection between happiness and income, and happiness and marriage. Here are some recent research findings about happiness. The name of the researcher is listed before the finding.

Evidence that money increases happiness

Layard: Increased income makes poor individuals happier.
Ahuvia: For non-poor people, differences in income can cause a 2 percent difference in feelings of well-being.

Evidence that money does not increase happiness

Layard: Increase in income does not make *non-poor* people happier.

Meyers: Money does not increase happiness for people who have necessities.

In the past 50 years, average U.S. incomes have doubled and:

- there are twice as many cars per person
- people eat in restaurants $2\frac{1}{2}$ times more often,

But:

- the percentage of people who are "very happy" has decreased from 35 to 32 percent
- teenage suicide has tripled
- violent crime is four times more frequent

Evidence of the factors that make marriage successful

Gottman: People are happier in relationships when they:

- Know about each other's needs and wants
- Use humor to help with stressful situations

Evidence that marriage makes people happier

Gottman: When people are happy or neutral about their marriage, they are generally happier than other people.

American Psychological Association: Married people are 1 percent happier than nonmarried people.

ACTIVITY **11** **Making claims in a discussion**

Work in a small group. Use the roles from Chapter 1 for participating in groups. Each person in your group will make a claim about an issue in the "The Gift of the Magi." You may choose a claim from the list on page 166, or you can make your own claim. Provide evidence to support your claim. You can use evidence from above, from the story, or your own evidence.

Take notes about your issue, claim, and evidence, and then summarize each. Here is an example of some notes:

Issue: What conn. betw. money and successful relationship?
Claim: Jim and Della can be happy without money.
Evidence:
 Not much money:
  apt not nice
  clothes not new
  not many possessions
 Not poor:
  Jim has job
  apt
  food: chops
Success: Have important thing: sacrifice for other: each gave up most important thing to make other happy

Here is an example of an oral summary about the claim. (Notice that the speaker uses simple present tense to discuss evidence from the story.)

An issue in "The Gift of the Magi" is the connection between money and love. I think that Jim and Della can be happy even though they do not have money. They know what is important in a relationship.

First of all, it is true that they have money problems. Their apartment is not that nice, and they do not have nice clothes. They don't have a lot of possessions. But I don't think they are really poor. They have enough food to eat. They have a place to live. They have enough money to be happy.

Gottman says that what makes people successful in a relationship is understanding what is important to their partner. Jim and Della are generous with each other. Even though they cannot use their gifts, they show that the other person is important by making a sacrifice of their most important possession. This means that they can be happy together.

Master Student Tip

When you are giving your point of view in a discussion, use rules of politeness to avoid insulting your listeners. People are more likely to listen to your ideas if they believe you respect them.

☐ Social Rules for Using Language: Politeness

Chapter 4 includes information about social rules, including rules for saving face for another person. (*Face* is the positive idea or image a person would like to have in the eyes of others.) A discussion among classmates is an example of a situation in which these rules can be used. When students discuss issues and claims, they may agree and disagree. A disagreement in a discussion is a good example of a situation that can cause another person to lose face. Although students in this situation are equal in status, they may not know each other well. This means they are more likely to use politeness rules when they disagree. Here are some rules that English speakers use to avoid causing another person to lose face when they disagree:

- focus on your own views, not the disagreement

   I don't see it that way.

   I have a different idea.

- concession: if possible, agree with part of another person's view

   Part of what you say is true, but I don't agree that . . .

   Yes, but what about . . .

   That's a good point, but . . .

- express comprehension if you cannot agree

   I see what you're saying, but . . .

ACTIVITY 12 **Practicing polite disagreement in a discussion**

Work with a partner. Choose one of the statements below. Practice disagreeing with the statement. When you explain your disagreement, use evidence from "The Gift of the Magi," and also politeness rules, including expressing comprehension, making concessions, and focusing on your own views.

- Money is more important than love in a relationship.
- Della and Jim can never be happy because they are poor.
- Della and Jim were foolish in their choice of gifts.
- Money can help any relationship succeed.

ACTIVITY 13 **Responding to claims in a discussion**

In this activity, you will respond to claims about money and happiness. Work in a group, and use the roles for group participation from Chapter 1. Read each statement. Respond by agreeing or disagreeing. Provide evidence to persuade your listener that you are right. You may want to use evidence from pages 167–168 or examples from your own experience. If you disagree, use the politeness rules including expressing comprehension, making concessions, and focusing on your own views.

1. Here is a quote from the book *The Gospel of Wealth* by Andrew Carnegie. Carnegie became one of the richest men in America in the late 1800s. He was the founder of U.S. Steel, a giant industrial corporation:

   As a rule, there is more genuine satisfaction, a truer life, and more obtained from life in the humble cottages of the poor than in the palaces of the rich. I always pity the sons and daughters of rich men, who are attended by servants, and have governesses at a later age, but am glad to remember that they do not know what they have missed.

   Respond to Carnegie's claim that the poor are happier than the rich.

2. Here is a quote from the book *Declarations of Independence*, by Howard Zinn, in which the author describes the contrast between rich and poor in the United States:

   Staggering technological advance alongside poverty and hunger. A class of extremely rich people; another class of quite prosperous people (but nervous about the security of their situation); another class of men, women, and children living in desperation and misery within sight of colossal wealth. Who could be surprised that crime, violence, and drug addiction would accompany such contrasts? Or that psychic disorder, broken families, and alcoholism would accompany such insecurity?

   From *Declarations of Independence; Cross-examining American Ideology*, by Howard Zinn 1990, Harper Collins.

   Respond to Zinn's claim that the difference between rich and poor causes social problems such as violence and drug addiction.

Here is an example for number 1:

I disagree with Carnegie. I don't believe that the poor have more satisfaction than the rich. Studies show that poor people are not as happy as other people.

It is true that money doesn't make you happy by itself. For example, people have more money now than they did fifty years ago, and people are not happier in general. However, money *does* make the poor happy.

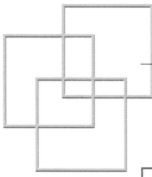

Part 3

ASSESSING YOUR ACADEMIC LISTENING AND SPEAKING SKILLS

☐ Listening to a Short Talk

 ACTIVITY 14 **Taking notes while listening to a talk**

Listen to the talk about the handout that follows. As you listen, take notes on the handout. When you finish, your instructor will test you on what you heard.

Lit I
Prof. Joyce
Spring semester

Writing a Persuasive Paper in Response to Literature

Steps:

1. State an **issue**.
2. Make a **claim** about an issue. A claim is "a statement that is made in the hope that it will be considered true."
   When you state a claim about an issue, you have written a **thesis statement** for your persuasive paper, a statement of the main or central idea in your paper.
3. **Persuade** your audience about your claim. When you persuade, you must **consider your audience**, that is, make an argument that considers what you know about the people who are reading or listening to what you say. Also, you must **provide evidence**, that is, observations or facts that support your claim.

ACTIVITY 15 **Using notes to prepare a summary**

Review your notes from Activity 13, and prepare to summarize the talk. Your instructor might ask you to give your oral summary in a small group or to the whole class.

☐ **Assessing Your Speaking**

ACTIVITY **16** **Getting feedback on your speaking skills**

Your instructor may use this checklist to discuss your use of academic English in your speaking assignments.

	OK	Needs work	Example(s)
Content:			
■ summarized the main points in a persuasive paper			
■ gave examples for main points			
Vocabulary:			
■ used academic vocabulary appropriately			
■ used paraphrases to make meaning more clear			

☐ Self-Assessment

ACTIVITY 17 **Evaluating your progress**

Review this list of chapter objectives. Think about your work and progress in each of these areas. Make a check mark after objectives that need your special attention in future work on academic speaking and listening.

- Take notes on a class handout _____

- Understand paraphrases _____

- Respond to arguments: agreeing and disagreeing _____

- Persuade an audience about issues, claims, and evidence _____

WEB POWER

You will find additional exercises related to the content in this chapter at **http://esl.college.hmco.com/students**.